101 WINNING BASKETBALL CONCEPTS & STRATEGIES

A COACH'S GUIDE FOR PLAYERS AND COACHES

101 WINNING BASKETBALL
CONCEPTS & STRATEGIES

A COACH'S GUIDE FOR PLAYERS AND COACHES

Mike McDonnell

Butler Books

ISBN: 978-1-953058-89-8

Printed in the United States of America

Book design by Scott Stortz

Published by:
Butler Books
www.butlerbooks.com

Coach Mike McDonnell has come up with a serious instrument to elevate your game, whether referencing coaches or players. I thoroughly enjoyed *101 Winning Basketball Concepts & Strategies* because it was born out of sweat, tears, and years. Each segment brings forth ideas experimented with and honed with a career spanning over 40 seasons. The anecdotes make the concepts and strategies crystal clear and enjoyable to read. Coach McDonnell is right when he says that the more a coach can say "always" or "never," the greater the clarity. No matter where you are in your career, this is a great read. Congrats Coach!

> — *Bob Cimmino, Mount Vernon High School boys' varsity basketball coach, all-time leader in Section 1 wins with 694, 8 Class AA titles*

A different way to focus on the fundamentals of the game will open terrific avenues for player improvement, and this book provides that.

> — *Bob Walsh, St. John's head of basketball operations and former University of Maine head coach*

Coach Mike McDonnell's *101 Winning Basketball Concepts & Strategies* is an amazing collection of simple, easy-to-understand ideas, tidbits, and stories from the 40-year career of one of New York's elite coaches. This enjoyable book includes fascinating insight into the teaching of the game for all levels, and details real experiences that cemented his methods. McDonnell's work is a must read for any aspiring coach who wants to master their craft!

> — *Scott Wright, Suffern High School boys' varsity basketball coach, who led Suffern to the greatest season in school history: 21–2 in 2018–2019*

CONTENTS

FOREWORD

As a 30-year Division I baseball coach, it's clear and easy to see where this journey began for me. But little did I know, as a 10-year-old, that I was getting a tutorial in coaching: yellow pads; phone calls with players, coaches, and parents; other coaches always in the kitchen or living room talking plays and strategies; and daily rides to practices and games. But it was not just me; it felt like the entire team was being picked up and brought home after practices and games. Two things were clear:

1. Mike's love of basketball and coaching.
2. His ability to help kids find joy in hoops while learning this great game.

Many youth teams are coached by a teammate's dad. I was getting coached by a big brother who was beginning his journey in coaching. You see, he didn't fade out when I aged out. He was in this for a lifetime, and he started just as I was entering youth sports. The blessing for me was that he was starting a 40+ year coaching career, and I got to witness it, experience it, and live it up close and personal. It's why when my playing career came to an end, I desired to give coaching a shot. Could I find as much joy in coaching as my brother did? Could I not just help others but find a purpose in teaching the game to them? Would they love the sport as much as I do? Would they want to win as much as I did? Why not?

They did for my brother. And if you love the game of basketball and desire to help others, this is the book for you.

—Dan McDonnell, University of Louisville baseball coach, *named 2x National Coach of the Year*

INTRODUCTION

Beginnings

It is 1979 and I am a 10th grade student at Iona Prep, New Rochelle, New York. The prior year, I was cut trying to make the freshman team. My elementary school, Our Lady of Mercy, runs its annual high school tournament in Port Chester, NY, in a cramped CYO (Catholic Youth Organization) gym, the first week of April each year, and I have just decided to join our varsity team and *coach* them. For 50 years, this tournament has drawn the best players from New York City, Westchester, Long Island, Rockland, NY, New Jersey, and Fairfield, CT.

Growing up, I witnessed, in this tiniest of gyms, supremely talented players like Butch Lee, who went on to win a national championship at Marquette, Jamal Mashburn, Felipe López, Hands McMillan, Tony "Red" Bruin, Roderick Rhodes, Vern Fleming, Bobby Hurley Jr., Danny Hurley, Lloyd Daniels, Chris Mullin, Pearl Washington, Kenny Smith, Walter Berry, John Salley, Ed Pinckney, Lamar Odom, Elton Brand, Speedy Claxton, Billy Goodwin, and so many other greats. Throughout my formative years, I witnessed this superior show of basketball talent annually, from a stage overlooking the court, with the benches just a foot or two below my feet. Imagine being a 10-year-old boy and almost touching the players! Other spectators packed the benches courtside, with their feet inbounds. The tang of the polyurethane-waxed floor, mixed with the old wood and painted concrete of my surroundings, alerted my nose that everything was perfect in the world, for this was the smell of basketball in *my* gym.

The two rival Amateur Athletic Union (AAU) powerhouses in NYC were Riverside Church and the Gauchos, but other teams like the Madison Square Boys Club and Westchester All Stars had some special moments, as well. I still remember witnessing—as a 10-year-old—Albert King, the brother of the great Bernard King, taking his second-place trophy and smashing it against the wall in the narrow locker room after losing to Ty Ladson and the boys from Canarsie High School in Brooklyn. The day before, the director of CYP (Catholic Youth Program), Bill Gallagher, had tossed me and a few other boys out of that same locker room for flipping quarters against the wall. (The person who tossed the quarter closest to the wall won the round and collected the quarters.)

The Our Lady of Mercy tournament has traditionally hosted two divisions: the Closed Division, consisting of high school teams from a single town or high school, and the Open Division which brings in the very best players from anywhere the coach putting the team together pleases. I've joined the varsity team of Iona Prep, a school that would later graduate Ty Jerome, a national champion point guard at the University of Virginia and eventually an NBA pro. The Closed Division followers, or at the very least, the CYP Director, are looking forward to a final game between Scarsdale and Mount Vernon, which have battled all season for Class AA Section 1 supremacy and are now on course to meet again. During the regular season, Scarsdale is coached by the great Jack Kaminer. Mount Vernon is the perennial powerhouse, one that graduates future college and NBA players including Gus and Ray Williams, and Rodney and Scooter McCray. Scarsdale is led by six-foot-eight John Revelli, who is heading to Stanford, and a talented two-guard in Butch Graves, who is committed to Yale.

The Iona Prep varsity is a .500 team this year, with no Ty Jeromes, exactly; but the very discipline-driven Brother Jensen has led a group of talented young men to compete in the tough New York State Catholic High School Athletic Association (NYCHSAA). The regular season is over now, so Brother Jensen isn't coaching them in this tournament.

Here I am in white carpenter jeans and a T-shirt, calling timeouts and trying to assist our varsity in any way I can, despite the seeming absurdity of it. We are seeded eight to Scarsdale's one and are expected to be just a first-round, easy road bump to the eventual matchup between the two Section 1 New York public school basketball forces, Mount Vernon and Scarsdale. We mess up that plan by beating Scarsdale in the opening game in overtime. We lose, eventually, in a very competitive championship game versus Mount Vernon, but a spark that was already well lit in me grows brighter. My coaching career has begun. It is the spring of 1979, and I have just turned sixteen.

The Gauchos

More than twenty years after my CYP tourney introduction to coaching, I have already assisted in college and been a head high school coach, with mixed results, at best. During the summer of 2000, after a rough season as the head high school boys' coach in Somers, NY, the father of Steve Masiello Jr. (the current associate head coach at St. John's University and former Manhattan College coach) says to me, while serving a succulent rib-eye steak off his grill, "Mike, you need to go down to the Gauchos, meet Fred Neal, and coach down there."

Throughout the 1980s and '90s, the Gauchos and Riverside Church Hawks were recognized as the best AAU programs in the New York metro area, and NYC produced the best talent in the country. Many of the young stars mentioned in my CYP tourney-coaching baptism played for the Gauchos at some point in time. Steve Masiello was sold on the Gauchos, enough to make sure that his son, Steve Masiello Jr., joined the program during his sophomore year at Archbishop Stepinac High School. His father knew that Steve's Harrison, NY, suburban-style game, though good, would greatly benefit from playing inner-city ball against the best from Manhattan, Brooklyn, Queens, and the Bronx. Dad was right; his son's overall game developed rapidly.

I take up Steve's offer and drive some 20 minutes from my Yonkers home, down the Major Deegan Parkway and past the old Yankee Stadium on my left, through the Hunts Point Market, arriving at the hallowed gym on Gerard Avenue. I knock on a door and briefly disrupt the meeting of five coaches by shoving my interrupting head into their peace and serenity. Ten eyes fixate on me, wondering who this 36-year-old, skinny, Caucasian interloper is, and I mumble, "Steve sent me to see Fred Neal?" An even thinner, bald-headed Fred Neal replies, "I am going to be in this meeting another 40 minutes. *Go and start practice.*"

What?! All right, this is *game time.* I quickly gather my thoughts in front of the three steps that lead to the expansive court and think of the first three drills that I will run. If I can just get through the first three drills, I know I will keep the practice rolling. I soon climb those stairs, scanning the large airport-hangar gym where I witness teenagers and young men strewn around and focusing on their individual improvement. Their tattoos and their determination hit me immediately. I parade to midcourt, blow a whistle, and a few heads turn before the players quickly return to what they were doing, as if a gnat has nipped at their necks. A much louder shriek of my whistle immediately follows, and I croak: "Let's go! Everyone in. Bring it in!" They slowly begin to make their way to half-court. I make an incoherent introduction. "Fred Neal. . . blah. . . blah. . . let's get to it."

That was my introduction to city basketball. It would forever positively change the way I viewed the game. *I would never coach the same again.*

Gaucho ball, or city-ball style, was running sets like four-low and getting the ball to the *tin*. To the *RIM*. We ran three-man weaves into four-low and would put a defender who was already in foul trouble on an island. Almost every player could handle the *ROCK*. We pressed the whole game, changing presses from 2-1-2, 2-2-1, and 1-3-1 back to man defense. Your best offensive player would be "in lock"—one aggressive defender would hound that player all game long. We ran quick-hitter plays out of box sets, but our best offense (besides our fast break and conversions off steals) was just getting the ball up on the glass and going and getting it. When we played very good teams, like the Long Island Lightning, filled with tough, talented Catholic school players from Long Island, I could appreciate the vast differences in approach. The mostly white, committed Long Island players ran Princeton-style flair screens and rapid-motion three-point shooting offenses, while our group of mostly black players from NYC, Queens, and Brooklyn, played the style I mentioned.

The Lightning might hit ten three-pointers to our one three-pointer, yet we would win most times. Each team would be extremely well coached and play in the style that best suited the team, but a vision began to emerge within my coaching psyche. What if I could blend the city style and lessons learned at the Gauchos with the suburban methods that I had utilized in the past? A hybrid. Play a style that took the best from both worlds. *Yes!*

That summer I coached players like Bevon Robin, the star guard at Fordham University, and God Shammgod, the NYC ballhandling wizard and Lasalle Academy graduate who led Providence to an Elite 8 in 1997 and played for the Washington Wizards in the NBA. I was the coach of the college players for two summers, but the most impactful and desirable coaching position was the prep school coach of rising high school seniors, and that was run by Robert Holford. I ended up assisting Coach H the entire summer of 2000. He was bringing the Gauchos back to relevance after a decline in the late '90s, due to a scandal with the previous founder of the organization. "H" was the man to do it. Rob and director Paul Brown recruited some of the best players in the NY metro area, including Royal Ivey (University of Texas and NBA), Julius Hodge (NC State and NBA), Roscoe Biggers (leading scorer in NYC out of Wadleigh HS and Baylor), Ryan Williams (Cardozo HS, Queens, St. Johns, Special FX of the And1 Tour), and many more. In one game at the very competitive Queens IS8, Coach H had me cover the game for him, and I coached five players over six feet seven. My coaching mentality was always to be prepared for the worst, so I feared blowing a game with all this talent, and I was ready from the tipoff—for all of three minutes, because we were already leading 17–2. *Sit down you foolish, foolish coach and relax for once. No, sit down. And don't move. This is a rap!*

Even though I was the only Caucasian coach during the two summers I spent with the Gauchos, I was never looked at differently by anyone, be it player or coach. In the basketball world, and in city basketball especially, people respect passion and knowledge for the game. I love that basketball has taken me to different places and helped me to meet people of different cultures. I loved that after a Friday night practice at the Gaucho Center, there was nothing better than to cross the 145th Street Bridge with Coach H and grab some soul food at the famous Sylvia's in Harlem, or stop off for some Jerk Chicken at a Jamaican deli. I happen to be a mix of Puerto Rican, Italian, English, and Irish, but my real race is Orange. I belong to the orange race of people who are obsessed with the great game of hoops.

REFLECTION

Over 40 years after my CYP beginnings, I am still coaching, and loving it more than ever. I've been blessed to work with some amazing young men and women through the years. My journey has included more than 300 high school varsity head-coaching victories, WNBA scouting, head college coaching for five years at the New York Empire State Summer Games, and college assistant-coaching stints in Florida and New York, along with many CYO and AAU experiences.

For me, coaching is about teaching and inspiring individual and team growth, and this book is completely dedicated to that principle. Establishing relationships and building trust between players, parents, and coaches form the bedrock that will allow for players and parents to be receptive to the fundamental teachings that I will illuminate throughout this book. More than any league title, I remember summers spent with high school players at camps like the St. Joseph's Phil Martelli Team Camp in Philadelphia, PA, hiding under a pile of leaves while playing manhunt at night on the main campus; or Ramapo College Team Camp in Mahwah, NJ, the annual Fordham University Team Camp in the grand old Rose Hill Gymnasium; or preseason trips with my suburban Putnam Valley players into Bedford-Stuyvesant, Brooklyn, to toughen the boys. Those trips and times spent together in the offseason were more rewarding to me than the season itself.

Effective coaching begins with communication and relationships. The best coaches teach young people the numerous skills and fundamentals of the game; the methods, pride, and thrill of competing; and the need to put group goals ahead of individual ones. When the aforementioned is achieved in a caring and fun environment, there is nothing better. Simply, it is best when players are having fun and truly looking forward to practices and games.

Coaching basketball has been the great privilege of my life. There are many extremely bright, dedicated, and talented high school coaches in the NY metro area and its surrounding suburbs, and my value and respect for my opponents and coaching peers makes me value each win. The vast majority of my coaching peers are wise and learned in the game, and their passion for basketball and leadership is apparent. I know that there are few secrets in this age of scouting and YouTube, and so I turn to two main concepts as my guiding principles:

1. Teach the players throughout the entire program to play in your fundamental system and style while adapting to the talent on hand. In high school, this changes each year.

2. Win the day. Simply outwork your opponents in the spring, summer, fall, and winter. No tricks. No secrets.

The great Glenn Frey of the iconic American band the Eagles once described his maturation as a singer and songwriter following the lessons being taught in the apartment just below his by a young singer-songwriter who awoke each morning at seven o'clock and began to hone his craft. His name was Jackson Browne ("Doctor My Eyes"). Frye described the secret of Browne's success poetically, as a songwriter would: "So that's how you do it. Elbow Grease. Time. Thought. Persistence." Should it be any different in basketball?

The Mission

Here are 101 approaches to more fundamentally prepared players, coaches, and teams. Winning basketball games results from winning habits of play. This book delivers instruction and insights into the most important habits leading to victory. My own Top 10 maxims begin the list. I repeat my Top 10 over and over to players; they serve as a springboard to team identity. These Top 10 are reinforced in several ways: through the spoken word, drills, and by immediately stopping practice when they are not followed. Players quickly understand whether *you say what you mean and mean what you say* or show moderate appreciation for certain behaviors but rarely follow up. Coaches, you need to make up your own Top 10. You may choose some of my principles/maxims or none at all. But that list needs to be made.

Focus on the fundamentals, NOT just on plays and sets. The fundamentals will help to develop players with high basketball IQs and propel them to maybe even compete in college, one day. This book is unique; I rarely hear these concepts taught to players in a consistent and persistent manner. I've been blessed to have learned from great people and have no conceit in this area, rather I want to share this knowledge with you. I've been so blessed, and thus I feel a responsibility to share with coaches, parents, and boys and girls of all ages.

Throughout the book, I will designate timeouts and anecdotes of memorable moments and people I've encountered along my coaching journey. I have grouped the concepts and strategies into categories to assist you in retracing areas you may most want to focus upon. This book applies to players of all ages, boys and girls, from grammar school to professional levels, for training in fundamentals and raising basketball IQs are needed at all levels. I am especially excited to begin a new career coaching on the girls' side of the sport at Briarcliff High School for the 2023–24 season. Who will benefit most from this book? Players, coaches, and parents.

My Top 10

1. CATCH AND SIGHT RIM.

Every time you catch the ball, immediately *sight rim*. Don't dribble to the land of nowhere or dribble and lose sight of the fact that you have a post player with position who is open and ready to receive. Don't catch and travel. *CATCH AND SIGHT RIM.* Against a press, *catch and sight rim.* In the half-court, you may be open and have the shot. You can't shoot at what you don't see, so sight rim. Catch and be ready to shoot. Catch and be ready to pass to an open teammate. None of these happen if your head is down and you are dribbling. Stop peeing with the ball. This isn't a dribbling show.

Coaching Exception:

Against a poor closeout, you are ready to drive and attack the rim immediately off the catch, *BUT* you still sight the rim. Coaches, be persistent in demanding that your players sight the rim each and every time. Stop practice every time, until your players own the concept.

2. NEVER DRIBBLE A LOOSE BALL.

Never dribble a loose ball. Pick it up, secure it immediately, and sight rim. When you try to advance a loose ball, you will often get it re-stolen from behind. The more times we can say always or never as coaches, the greater clarity and emphasis we give to the way our players approach the game. *AT* [plug in name of your school] *WE NEVER DRIBBLE A LOOSE BALL.* We never dribble a loose ball!

3. PITCH AHEAD.

Follow our *FIRST OPEN-PLAYER RULE* and pass ahead to the first player you see open ahead of you. The ball moves faster through the air than any sprinting ball handler can. Pass ahead. Catch, sight rim, and pass ahead. We are totally committed to transition, and we run an air break—a fast break where the ball moves primarily through the air. *Pitch ahead* is a short phrase that coaches can chirp anytime they see players failing to pass ahead to that first open player.

Coaching Exception:

A team may have the one jet-quick point guard whom you designate as the blow-it-up-via-the-dribble option. You may have a talented post player who starts the break via the dribble blowout.

4. HOT COALS! HOT COALS!

You have three seconds to sprint through the hot coals which exist (in our minds) between foul lines. Visualize your feet burning on hot coals if you don't get through the area in three seconds or less. It is not: *jog* through the hot coals. It is not: sprint one possession, take it easier on the next possession. Go all out and ask for a sub as soon as you realize you have hit the wall. Don't worry, because as coaches, we see immediately when you are not sprinting. We can't be a running team if *you* are jogging. Old people go for a jog. Not basketball players. We are committed to the missed and made basket break. It begins with our commitment to getting through those burning hot coals. Wings, run hard and run wide. Wings, run wide just six inches inside your left or right lane. This concept was taken from a great book called *Stuff Good Players Should Know: Intelligent Basketball from A to Z,* by Dick DeVenzio (2nd ed. Austin: Bridgeway Books, 2006. See "The Race Track," 122), and the concept of sprinting from foul line to foul line in less than three seconds is centered around the approach to *BOTH* offensive and defensive transition.

Coaching note: Language is power.

When coaches use powerful images, such as burning coals, it helps players connect to a concept. Players have so much to think about. Powerful imagery can break through a player's game fog. A simple reminder such as *"HOT COALS. . . HOT COALS!"* jolts players into active sprinting.

5. SELECT GOOD SHOTS.

Good shot selection is a must. I remind my players all the time that *a bad shot is as good as a turnover*. We work together to get quality open looks from the outside, tough drives to the basket, and feeds into the post. Off-balance shots, challenged shots, and hope-and-prayer shots are death to an offense. Absolute killers. The quickest way to sit on a bench is poor shot selection. Do not take "my turn" shots. Do not shoot challenged shots. A drive is going to be challenged, of course, but there is no excuse for shooting strongly contested, perimeter shots.

6. WIN THE WAR OF THE BOARDS.

Players, take pride in your rebounding. Guards, you are critical to defensive rebounding, especially in this era of basketball where long threes bounce off and become 50/50 balls. Do you have the nose and desire to win those balls? Most rebounds in high school, and in age levels below high school, are secured below the rim. Boxing out is not new to anyone, yet it never gets old. Fundamentally speaking, make contact with a firm forearm shiver (contact thrust) into your opponent's chest. Keep your elbows above your shoulders.

The defensive rebounder can do the footwork in one of two ways: front-facing step across or drop, step, and cut off the angle of the offensive rebounder, using the drop-pivot move. I teach both. Just be physical and get the job done. The goal is to drive the offensive rebounder a stride or two away from the basket. If you are consistently getting fouled with a hockey-style crosscheck, you may need to sell that you are being fouled, but that is a gamble.

When considering offensive rebounding, the technique we taught at Rye was to SOFO (DeVenzio, *Stuff Good Players Should Know*, 16). Spin Off the First Object and avoid going over the back of the box-out. Another effective offensive rebounding technique is to wedge the defensive rebounder closer to the basket by placing one leg between his legs, jumping straight up, and trying to win the 50/50 ball or deflecting it out for possible possession.

7. BUST SOME PIPES BY APPLYING
RELENTLESS DEFENSIVE PRESSURE.

Pressure makes diamonds. Pressure busts pipes. Let's bust some pipes! At the Gauchos, we employed a NYC, relentless defensive-pressure mentality and forced turnovers to capitalize on. Now, some coaches might feel that they don't have more talent than the opponent and thus approach pressure differently, and that is understandable. However, there are many ways to exert pressure: full court, three-quarter court or half-court zone and man presses. I often favor zone presses back to half-court man defense. A coach can trap a basket-out-of-bounds (BOB) inbound pass out of a 2-3 zone. A coach may choose to apply a deny-defender tactic on one targeted player. A team may choose to trap every pick-and-roll with a call such as "Tornado" or " Red."

Exemplary Pressure-Defense Coach:
Tobin Anderson, Iona College.

Tobin Anderson is a coach who thrives on applying pressure after each made basket (and much more). Anderson coached Fairleigh Dickinson University to a most memorable 16 seed versus 1 seed victory over Purdue in the 2023 NCAA (National Collegiate Athletic Association) men's tournament. FDU was the shortest team in the entire tournament, and Purdue, led by seven-foot-four center Zach Edey, was one of the tallest—but speed, hustle, and relentless pressure busts pipes. Anderson is also able to teach his teams to apply great pressure without incessant, unnecessary fouling, which is not an easy accomplishment. Anderson is now ready to take that pressure mentality to Iona College and the MAAC (Metro Atlantic Athletic Conference), where he replaces Rick Pitino, who has moved on to Saint John's. Players, it is better to make a sin of commission than a sin of omission. In other words, be ready to jump a passing lane. Play bouncy, on the balls of your feet, and read where the most logical next pass will occur.

8. CASUAL LEADS TO CASUALTY.

My players often hear this refrain: "Casual leads to casualty." Don't let your guard down. Be focused. In high school, I also remind my players: "thirty-two minutes for a lifetime of memories." No style points. No reward for degree of difficulty. Make two-handed passes. Unfortunately, casual play even happens in the NBA. It is human nature. A player takes the ball out after a made basket and blindly inbounds to an opposing player, assuming it was his own teammate. Games are often decided by a point or two, and a casual misstep can cost your team the game.

Example: Casual Leads to Casualty in 2023.

The New York Yankees second baseman may have cost his team a June victory in the 2023 season with a glaring display of casual play. The Yankees had a one-run lead, late in the game, when a throw from the left fielder came into second base just a bit offline, and the second baseman did not even remotely move to catch the ball because he was trying to look cool. You know how this ends: The Red Sox tie and win in extra innings. Casual leads to casualty.

9. DO NOT SHOW THE BALL TO THE DEFENSE.

Protect the basketball. Don't tease the defense. If you get too cute, that ball will be swiped. Keep your body between the defense and the ball. If you don't have a wicked, low crossover that pulls the ball back off a staggered stance, not a parallel stance (for example, if you cross from left to right, your right foot should be a little behind your left and be shoulder width or a bit more apart), then don't rely on the cross to change directions. NBA players work continually on the low crossover, and their overall hand speed and ball manipulation. I've seen Division I, high-level perimeter basketball players succeed without using a crossover. In the first round of the 1996 NCAA tournament, Coach Pete Carril's Princeton team upset UCLA, the defending national champions, with perimeter players who rarely used a crossover. Remember, I coached at the Gauchos AAU and love NYC guards, so I am not against the crossover in any way, *for those who truly have a strong, competent crossover move.*

Exemplary NBA Player: Jalen Brunson, NY Knicks.

In today's game, I absolutely love to watch Jalen Brunson of the NY Knicks. He is my favorite player to study, for he thrives without having extraordinary physical attributes. Yes, he utilizes the crossover and a myriad of moves, but for this passage I want to focus on how he keeps his body between the defender and the ball. He gets super low coming off a ball screen. He utilizes a pullback dribble as he continues *to always protect the ball.* In our league this past year, we played against two very athletic teams in Ossining High School (Obi Toppin's high school) and White Plains High School. In our Horace Greeley scouting report, particularly against Ossining, I told our perimeter players: *NO CROSSOVERS. Put that move to bed for this opponent.* I had just scouted Ossining, which stole the ball numerous times playing White Plains earlier that week. One defender, in particular, had some of the quickest hands I had seen in a long time. We ended up losing by three points to Ossining, yet we gave ourselves a chance to win because we had few turnovers, no live-ball turnovers, and the boys followed the game plan.

Bonus Coaching Tip:

A loss does not mean that the adjustments you made for a game were ill-advised. Wise adjustments will improve your performance, but not guarantee a victory. If you've gone into a game as the underdog, you might have gotten blown out without the adjustments. Simply, you are trying to put your team in the best position to win.

10. PREVENT LIVE-BALL TURNOVERS.

Live-ball turnovers lose games. We can live with a dead-ball turnover. For example, we are being pressed and we throw the ball to the outside hand, up the sideline, and it goes out of bounds. *We can then set up our defense.* But a live-ball turnover often nets a negative four to six points. We don't score on one end, and a team goes the other way and scores without us being able to set up our defense. *NO LIVE-BALL TURNOVERS.* Coach Rob Holford would teach our offensive college wings who were at half-court against a press not to flash in a straight line to the ball, but rather to v-cut in, away from the sideline, moving toward the ball, then back toward the sideline. If we happened to throw the ball away there, it would have to be to the outside. He was adamant about *NO LIVE-BALL TURNOVERS.*

TIMEOUT: MY TWO GREAT MENTORS

This book would never have happened without these two coaches. Because of them, I focus on fundamentals and player development first and foremost, and then address offensive and defensive sets second. Many coaches do the reverse.

COACH JIM KELLY

Coach Kelly is my first prized mentor, from my early coaching years. He was a most successful high school boys' coach at Rye High School from the mid-1980s through the early 1990s, leading Rye to a state final in 1989. He is the reason I approach the game in a conceptual, fundamental way, a way that forms a basketball language with one's program or team. A great irony is that as I get older, I find myself going back and more deeply coaching in many of the methods I first learned as a teenage coach.

I am an 18-year-old winning many CYO tournaments at the Corpus Christi Youth Center in Port Chester, NY, which borders Greenwich, CT. I'm being well paid for what I would do for free, driving a church van, and coaching four CYO teams at one time, when my old CYO coach, Joe Vizzari, says to me, "If you *really* want to learn coaching, there is a coach at Rye High School who is special, and you really need to go work for him"—so I did. I am now 19 and barely older than the players I coach. I have seen Coach Jim Kelly take a program from 10–10 to 14–6, to a sectional title, and to an eventual state championship game. I still utilize what I learned from him about coaching. To this day, Jim and I communicate three to four times each week, via FaceTime. I often call Jim at 7:00 a.m., New York time, and connect with him at 1:00 p.m. in his locale, for he resides in Denmark.

In the summer of 2018, I visited Jim and was the guest clinician in Svendborg, Denmark, at a professional club called the Svendborg Rabbits. The program worried about potential compensation demands from this US-coaching friend of Jim's. I came at a cheap price: a hoodie and T-shirts to bring home were healthy enough compensation for me. The real reward was time spent with Jim as he showed me Copenhagen and the beauty of Denmark. I even experienced a Catholic mass in Vietnamese. That was by accident, as I misread mass times in Danish, and I still smile thinking of the number of congregants taking subtle glances at me in the back pew. Months later, Jim would reveal to me that he was losing his sight, and he soon went blind. No complaints. He lives a "yes-I-can spirit" every day. He sees the game so clearly in his mind that I run through my entire 2022–23 season at Horace Greeley, and he shares incredible insights and ideas to my immediate situations.

I worked for three years with Jim Kelly at Rye High School before moving to Tampa, FL, and coaching junior college basketball at Hillsborough Community College and St. Petersburg Junior College. Kelly taught me every aspect of being a high school coach. He was married to the game, and his approach was completely different from the approach of any other coach I have ever met. We would go out to eat, and he would spread out the sugar and ketchup packets to show the slides of a 2-2-1 press, and the show would begin. We would scrimmage, and he would do a running dictation of comments which I scribed to review with the players on the way home. I would read out loud something like this:

> 7:45 mark, first quarter: Ralph, first-open-man-rule pass to Greg. Excellent pass.
>
> 6:15: Greg, great bounce pass inside to Bobby for a layup. (Note: Rye players were taught to only bounce pass into the post, and Kelly drilled a post-entry-bounce-pass series daily, at practice.)
>
> 5:45: Bobby, great rim run. Guards, we missed him wide open.
>
> 5:20: Turnover pass by Paul. We don't throw one-handed passes. Why would you throw a one-handed pass? (in a tone that would make Paul feel as if he had personally offended and wounded him).
>
> We don't do that at Rye.

And this script would follow the entire scrimmage.

The result was that at Rye, the players were taught not just plays, sets, and team defenses, which is what 99 percent of coaches do, with light-to-medium emphasis on how to play. Rather, Jim emphasized playing the game in a prescribed manner that greatly increased our chances of winning, while at the same time still running very effective sets for offense and defense. Nobody was doing this. Nobody. Not to the extent that Jim was making his players utilize metacognition which means *thinking about thinking*. He taught players how to *think the game,* and our drills were aimed at forming *muscle memory,* so that players would behave in an almost instinctual way. That was the goal, and we had a method for everything, including foul shooting. Jim was a believer in *mental cybernetics* and positive thinking being preached by a successful high school coach in Brentwood, Long Island, named Stan Kellner. Stan ran the "Yes, I Can" camps. Players were given "Yes, I Can" stickers and more.

At Rye, our foul-line routine involved sighting the rim and seeing the ball swish through the net, followed immediately by saying the word *swish* silently, then bouncing the ball three times, looking up and saying *swish* again, with the same visualization, and then shooting. This all took five or six seconds. Jim even had a foul-shot technique for when a player felt overwhelmed by an end of game situation, be it nerves or a raucous crowd. He taught the player to look at the left corner of the backboard as a mind clearing device and then return to our standard routine prior to the shot. Bobby Latkany, who was a National Hotshot finalist as a nineth grader and our clutch 4-man (power forward), mastered getting to the foul line and made 21 of 22 shots in a state semifinal game to thrust Rye into a state final in 1989. Twenty-one of twenty-two! With the kind of detail Jim spent on foul shooting, you can imagine how well we were prepared for every aspect of the game.

This was the man I worked with, and how incredibly fortunate I was to learn from a high school coaching master. He once said to me, "I need you to scout Albertus Magnus on Saturday night," and he immediately picked up on my hesitation—I was 22 and thinking about my Port Chester friends, young ladies, and hitting the vibrant college bar scene on North Avenue in New Rochelle. His tone, which could make a person feel he had disappointed a priest in the confessional, straightened me out real fast.

"You want to be a coach, right? *This is coaching.*"

I never coached *mostly*-in again.

All successful coaches know how much they give up. They know how many holidays are filled with nursing a cold or flu or being distracted and more. We must love with energy and passion and be present for our loved ones for all those times we aren't fully there for them in mind and spirit.

COACH ROBERT HOLFORD

A coach on the rise, Robert Holford is invited to give a clinic on defense at Jack Curran's Five Star Basketball Camp. Clinics are given at one o'clock at the Curran camp, and the acoustics in Rose Hill Gymnasium can easily get lost, but not with Coach H. Holford is an assistant coach at Hofstra at a time when the names of two very young, emerging coaches are creating a buzz: one has the last name Calipari, and the other is Holford. Today at the camp, his boombox-intense voice resonates with a passionate crescendo as he demonstrates how an on-ball defender is like *"white on rice"*—and he proceeds to climb into a player's shorts. Did I just witness that?! I'm sold. This guy believes in his mission of teaching defense.

Ironically, I did not immediately connect that clinic appearance with the man before me at the Gauchos, fifteen years later. We soon became aware of each other, after I opted to assist him with his Gaucho Prep team (I continued to lead the college team), and my doctoral course in basketball had begun.

Coach Jim Kelly had brought me through my high school and undergraduate diploma. I led myself through a coaching master's program of sorts, through passion, trial, and error. But it was Robert Holford who would lead me through a doctoral program in coaching. When I went on to win five league titles in six years at Putnam Valley High School, Rob's influence would manifest itself throughout, but it all began at the Gauchos.

Holford ran NY-style, guard-oriented offenses such as three-guard spreads, during which our three guards would keep the ball away from the defense between the top of the key and half-court. These three-guard spreads would morph into 4-low calls, where the guard with the ball would play one-on-one in isolation, while his teammates were positioned along the baseline. We would run three-guard spreads into side pick-and-rolls called *slides* and truly maximize the great ballhandling talents that the NY metro area possessed. Holford would change presses from 2-2-2 to 2-1-2 and 1-3-1 full court, and so much more. He took out opposing best players with locks (a defender was told to take his defensive assignment out of the game, and he had *no help obligations*), and demanded that players win "The War of The Boards," as he came to call it. He mastered the art of skill development and had a fundamental teaching concept for every aspect of the game. He taught me to use every second available to be alone with the team and that you never have enough players. (On the Gauchos roster, we carried a rotating lineup of 18 players with 10 to 12 showing up on any weekend.) While other coaches were sleeping in our hotels, we were in the ballrooms walking through sets or parking lots with a garbage can for a hoop. He modeled basketball acumen, discipline, dignity, and love.

One night when I was assisting him at Hostos Community College, we were routing Ulster County Community College by almost 30 points in the first half. We had given up only 20 points. At halftime, Coach H tried to ensure that there would be no letdown by telling the players that if Ulster scored over 35 points, we would run a down-and-back sprint for every point over that marker. He knew we would assuredly win, but for Rob every game, every five-minute segment of a game, was an opportunity to push toward championship-level excellence. After a 30-minute post-game breakdown in the locker room, where about six "assistants" (any Hostos security guard who was given a clipboard and a T-shirt became an assistant) shared their thoughts on the game, the team was sent to the baseline with Coach McDonnell to run 17 down-

and-backs, despite winning by 55 points. Rob remained in the classroom as I led the victorious, yet annoyed young men, back to the court. There were a few grumbles, but this was city ball, and they knew that Coach H didn't play games.

In one practice, a player got himself into trouble and was sent to jog back and forth on the side, with the hope of rejoining the practice. I believe Coach H actually forgot about him, because he never rejoined the practice, and he jogged back and forth for over an hour. And take note: the player never dared to ask Coach H if he could rejoin the practice. To Rob, this is love: giving guidance and leadership to a group that will go on to win a national championship in D3 junior college, one year later, and learn that they have greatness within them.

This is the same man who hustled to the grocery store to buy enough chicken and rice for the entire team, for his wife Autumn to prepare a Friday team dinner at his home in Queens. The young men flooded his home from Manhattan, Brooklyn, the Bronx, and Queens, including Yabsa, a center from Senegal who, in order to pay the $4000 yearly tuition, as well as survive, sold various items strewn across a blanket he laid out on street corners in Manhattan. Yabsa would hit a top-of-the-key jumper to win the City University of New York (CUNY) city championship. Many coaches would not have had him shoot at all, yet Coach H always drilled his players to be ready to contribute when their number or situation came calling.

Reportedly, Yabsa is now living in Texas, owns two houses, and has two children. He is a Marine Corps sergeant. Rob has never become known like John Calipari, but I bet Yabsa wouldn't have gotten to where he is today without his growth as a person at Hostos Community College. Is the American Dream still alive? You're darn right it is.

Rob is love: Love of the game. Love of the preparation. Love of in-game coaching and adjustments. Love of people, and most especially his players. He adopted one teenage son, saving the boy from a life spent in foster care. One night this son, then an adult adorned by a fur coat that ended just below his waist, spoke about his plight, prior to Rob saving him from the devastating foster care system. The Hostos players and I choked up, the tears welling within me as I strove to keep it together.

Rob has been burned by many people in coaching, for the coaching world can be quite cruel. But I've never met a person who knew more about basketball than he does. Rob sometimes refers to our coaching tandem "salt-n-pepper." I love it, for any phrase that puts me in the same sentence with him is more than fine with me.

Ball Security

Teams that are sloppy or casual with the ball don't win. I am amazed at the casual and careless nature young players exhibit, and more jarring is the lack of instruction being given to them, as the urgent need to take excellent care of the basketball has not been instilled in them. It is not enough to say don't turn the ball over. In this section, fundamentals and ideas will be reviewed to make our handling of the basketball more secure, both individually and as teams.

11. IT TAKES TWO TO MAKE A TURNOVER.

It often takes two people to cost the team a turnover. Not all turnovers involve two guilty parties, but many do. I am coaching at Sacred Heart High School of Yonkers, and we are playing really well on the road against a larger school from Queens, Monsignor McClancy. The game goes down to the final seconds, and a center whom I have told to never inbound the ball after a made basket grabs the ball and attempts to inbound it. The ball gets stolen and we lose. Afterward, I speak with Coach Holford, who attended the game. I bemoan the result. "Sean turned the ball over. He's been told to *NEVER* take it out after a made basket." Coach Holford astutely observes that Christian, my freshman point guard, did not make himself clearly open to receive the pass.

"It takes two to make a turnover." I remind players of that all the time. Did you give a clear target? Did you make a strong v-cut to get open and show a target hand where you wanted the ball? Did you take steps to the ball to shorten the pass?

12. FIRE! A TEAMMATE IS TRAPPED: SPRINT TO THE BALL.

Anticipate traps. Yell *fire!* and sprint to the ball. When a teammate of yours is trapped, immediately sprint to the ball. How many times have you seen a player trapped while teammates stand flat-footed crosscourt waving their arms and saying, "I am open"? *YOU ARE NOT OPEN.* Good players anticipate when a teammate is in trouble and start to move before the trap even occurs. All four players need to flash to the ball: one player each to their teammate's immediate left, immediate right, center left, and center right.

Coaching Bonus Tip:

Run drills that teach the trapped player how to pivot and handle traps. Is it possible to throw a ball off a defender out of bounds? Use drills to teach players to sprint toward the ball.

13. NEVER DRIBBLE THE BALL OVER HALF-COURT VERSUS A MAN OR ZONE TRAP.

The ball handler must prevent being ridden up the sideline to pick up the dribble just over half-court. *Stop* before half-court and *reverse* the ball. Better yet, take a good pullback dribble and see if the reverse pass is open. The ball handler may pull back and find the middle man open. What probably won't be open is the ball-side sideline. If the player does dribble into a trap, a teammate may yell, *TIMEOUT,* especially if he plays for a coach who does not waste them, or he may yell *FIRE* and sprint to the ball, as mentioned earlier. Better yet, *DO NOT GET PUSHED UP THAT SIDELINE INTO A TRAP.* Pullback dribbles are vital against presses in both the backcourt and the frontcourt.

Player Bonus Tip:

If you sense you are in traffic when you receive an outlet pass, use the *quick glance backward technique* before speed dribbling ahead (rather than pitching ahead). Don't get the basketball stolen from behind. Only a speedy, secure ball handler is to use this technique. Others need to *pitch ahead.*

14. DON'T PASS TO A PLAYER WHO HASN'T REACHED THE DESTINATION.

Make sure that if a teammate is going from under the rim to an opening for a shot, be it to the corner or wing at the point line, you don't pass to that person on their way to the desired target area. Don't pass to them one to two strides off the baseline with their momentum going away from the basket.

What is the player to do with the ball? It is likely you will cause the person to travel. You may need to use a pullback dribble to buy more time or get low to keep your dribble alive until your teammate is ready to receive for an open shot. Do not hit your teammate with a pass just yet. Wait until your teammate has passed the three-point line or your teammate is curling, hands ready for an open wing or elbow two-point field goal attempt. Otherwise, you are going to force a turnover or break the flow of that specific offensive possession.

15. SHORTEN PASSES AND WORK TO GET OPEN.

The ball is being inbounded at half-court. You stand flat-footed, believing you are open. A defender cuts in front of you and takes the ball for an uncontested layup. You need to always shorten passes and move to get open. Take people two steps away and come hard to the ball. Take people a step to the ball and sprint backdoor. If you are posting up versus a press, meet a pass or shorten the pass by taking an extra stride toward the ball. We tell our posts: choose possession over keeping position. Give up position to keep possession.

16. USE THE KEVIN DOWNEY MOVE.

When you are handling the ball and facing defensive ball pressure, consider doing the following:

1. Turn your body sideways while still maintaining sight of the rim, thus keeping your body between the defender and the ball.

2. Use the non-dribbling arm and hand about a foot away from your body, keeping the defender away. Point the thumb of that hand to the floor.

3. Don't show the ball to the defense.

Exemplary Player: Kevin Downey.

Kevin Downey was a standout guard for the Canisius College Golden Griffins (Buffalo, NY) in the early 2000s and finished his career with over 1,000 points, 400 rebounds, and more than 250 assists. He played in the Empire State Summer Games for the western region (Buffalo area), and I coached against him as the head coach of the Hudson Valley team in the summer of 2005. He was a strong six-foot-three 2-guard, and as the son of a high school coach, played very fundamentally. I later watched him play against Iona College for Canisius and thought to myself: "What makes him so darn effective?" More than a few things of course. I took one key area away from watching him play: Kevin never showed the ball to the defense, using the aforementioned techniques. These are seemingly small fundamental actions, yet putting many fundamental actions together in a total package yields a high basketball-IQ player like Kevin Downey.

17. FAKE AND MAKE: UTILIZE STRONG PASS AND SHOT FAKES.

Fake and make. Don't underestimate the influence of a strong pass fake and its ability to move the defense in the wrong direction. Every advantage gained by the offense contributes to making more buckets and reducing turnovers, especially reducing live-ball turnovers. Pass fakes do not get the fans excited like dunks do, but they are very effective. In addition, do not stare down the intended target of your pass—very important to *not* make where you are passing the ball obvious. *Don't stare down your targets.* Periodically, look away from your intended target and make those quick, strong pass fakes. Shot fakes are a most effective tool, as well. Many players now shot fake and take a side dribble to stay behind the line and shoot the three without getting chased off the line. Shot fake, attack the rim. Shot fake, drive, and pullup. Shot fake and take a side or clearing dribble. Strong pass fakes and strong shot fakes are so effective.

Coaching Bonus Tip:

Players rush their fake and drive, so have them fake, count one second off, and then go. A neck cramp is not a shot fake. If the fake does not look like a shot, then it is not effective. Finally, I hate when posts fake a shot to the sideline or opposite basket. I will correct that immediately.

18. KEEP THE BALL IN PRIVATE PROPERTY.

You hear coaches tell post players to always keep the ball high—never bring it down. That is sound advice, for smaller guards lurk, waiting for you to bring the ball down. A six-foot-five player becomes four feet five with the ball down at the waist. But let's take this advice a step further: Get the ball to private property and assume somebody is *always* coming to take that ball. Not public property, but *private property,* as Gannon Baker, the accomplished basketball trainer, says. Absolutely. Move the ball to an area that might be off your left ear if you sense a defender on your right. Windshield-wipe the ball from one side to another. Give violent head fakes and secure the ball tightly with two hands. Assume somebody is always coming to block you, and learn to have that basketball sixth sense. Do not go up softly, get blocked, and act surprised. This isn't you dominating your classmates at lunchtime. You have competition. Why would the defense allow you free, unimpeded points? Be aware. Be tough. Be explosive.

19. SWITCH THE BALL AND KEEP IT LOW
TO AVOID THE SWIPE STEAL FROM BEHIND.

In the half-court, when you go by your defender, be aware of a last-ditch attempt by the defender to win the ball back. Quickly change hands and move the ball from the right hand to the left or vice versa, keeping the ball very low. After an exchange, you may pick up your dribble or continue to attack, but don't forget to move that ball.

20. PASS ONE STRIDE AHEAD,
NOT THREE STRIDES AHEAD.

After a steal, your lead pass needs to be one stride ahead, not three strides ahead. Players often overestimate the speed of their teammates or feel that they must overcompensate in leading a teammate to the basket. Nothing kills the momentum gained by a steal like giving the ball right back. It took too much work to get the ball; don't give it right back. One stride ahead is all you need. As I watched the 2023 Elite 8 game between Kansas State and Florida Atlantic University, a steal occurred, and the ball was thrown four strides ahead, out of bounds. One team went to a Final 4 and one team, Kansas State, went home after a three-point loss, 74–71. The little things matter. One stride ahead. One stride ahead.

21. CONCENTRATE ON YOUR FOOTWORK
TO AVOID TRAVEL VIOLATIONS.

Heel-toe. Heel-toe. Don't travel off the catch and first dribble. Concentrate on your footwork. Catch and have a definite pivot foot shifting weight from heel to toe. It is so frustrating to turn a ball over needlessly (not because of a trap), as a result of your own poor footwork. Don't give the officials awkward or unnecessary footwork that lacks purpose toward a drive. Keep it simple. Bend low, and on your first dribble, get the ball on the deck before you pick up the pivot foot. You can't run with the ball, so get it down.

22. DO NOT THROW MAYBE PASSES.

Your eyes don't lie. If you see that a potential pass is going to be a risky proposition, don't throw it. A 50/50 proposition is a *NO GO*. We want 90/10 and above propositions. If the shot clock is seven seconds or below, you may want to be riskier, but otherwise be smart, respect the basketball. A player may wave frantically at you, wanting you to throw the pass, but you can choose to ignore this. I'm not jumping off the Brooklyn Bridge with you. I see that you are not as open as you may think. If you continue to throw maybe passes, then you are going to get maybe playing time.

Coaching Bonus Tip:

When a player persists in throwing maybe passes, take the player out and sit her down next to your assistant coaches. After restating the teaching point, put the player back in the game. Even a one-minute removal reminds a player about your priorities.

23. KNOW YOUR TEAMMATE'S ABILITY
TO HANDLE CERTAIN PASSES.

What a perfect pass is for one player on your team may be disastrous for another. You need to know whether your teammate can handle the pass you are making. Some post players can't handle anything low. Some players can't catch well on the run. If you want to feed the ball to a post who is not holding position, why force it? They don't deserve the ball on that particular possession.

24. STAY OUT OF DANGER ZONES.

Danger zones include areas of the court where a turnover is more likely. If you are a physically explosive player, the baseline may suit you very well, but if you aren't, just remember you are adding a sixth defender (the out-of-bounds line) against you, and the defense is sinking into the paint. Teams cheat the baseline hammer pass to the opposite corner (the opposite wing is often more open than the corner). If you are slightly bumped—and you often will be on the baseline—and step out of bounds, the likelihood is that a foul *will not be called.* It is a good idea to always play six to eight inches inside the court, whether sideline or baseline. NBA pros accidentally step out of bounds quite often off skip passes. They at least have the excuse that the size and wingspan of NBA defenders is challenging enough that you need every inch of space. They should still be half a foot inside the line. One step over the half-court sideline is dangerous because you have no reversal option, and you have only one side of the floor that you can easily work with. The defense knows that.

25. GET TO CONTROLLED, TWO-FOOTED
JUMP STOPS IN THE PAINT.

When driving into the lane, get to a strong, on-balance, two-footed jump stop. Don't get too deep in the paint. One step inside the foul line is ideal.

Coaching and Player Exemplars: Jay Wright and Jalen Brunson.

Nobody did this better than Coach Jay Wright's Villanova teams. Get to a balanced two-foot landing with a wide, strong base, and be ready to pivot and keep the ball in private property as you look for open teammates or even end up ultimately pivoting your way into a shot. Nobody does this better than Jalen Brunson, the former Villanova Wildcat and current New York Knicks point guard. Brunson is a pivoting machine: a pivoting machine of up-and-under moves and 10-foot fadeaways.

Player Bonus Tip:

Being a fan of players like Lebron James or Kevin Durant is understandable, but their approaches to the game are not something you will likely mimic, because of your size. Instead, mirror the games of players like Steph Curry or Jalen Brunson. Study their bag of tricks. Go to YouTube and bring up videos of Steve Nash and Tony Parker. There is so much video available from past greats.

26. NEVER LIFT THE BALL INTO
THE UNDER-ARREST POSITION.

When under the duress from intensive defensive pressure, do not lift the ball into a stationary over-your-head position. That is the "you-are-under-arrest" or "give-me-your-valuables" position. Windshield-wipe the ball with a strong two-handed grip. Pivot, get low, and get your body between the defender and the ball. Try to avoid getting close to this position by thinking one pass ahead, one play ahead, and by being decisive. It is likely you ended up under arrest because you were playing around with the ball instead of keeping the ball moving. It is much better to avoid pitfalls than to have a hundred strategies for getting out of trouble.

27. HOW TO ESCAPE A DOUBLE TEAM.

With a left pivot foot, step out very low and far out to the right, windshield-wipe the ball over your head violently and step out as far as you can to the left. Reverse pivot back to the middle, and attempt to step through the opening that your previous two moves created. Finally, take the trap low by faking low and jump pass. This is one of the few times you are encouraged to leave your feet to make a pass. The only other leave-your-feet pass is to sell a short 12-to-14-foot runner that is a vertical lob to a waiting post player. Know the possession arrow because a jump ball is a victory for the offense if the possession arrow is in your favor. Finally, if you must, *EAT THE BALL* and take the five count. A dead-ball turnover is preferable to any live-ball turnover. Finally, a teammate or coach may demonstrably wave for a timeout.

28. STAY ON THE FLOOR FOR MOST PASSES.

It is dangerous to make passes in the air. Once you leave the floor, you are vulnerable to an up-and-down violation. Off the dribble, you see a teammate cutting backdoor and seemingly very open. At the last moment, you are surprised to witness a defender jump into the passing lane and your peripheral line of sight. This is not unusual; in basketball the battlefield changes rapidly. You want to abort the mission like NASA often does when they decide to delay a rocket launch, due to inclement weather. *BUT YOU CAN'T.* You left the floor. Why?

Exceptions to this fundamental:

Off a drive, you may leave your feet to throw a "push shot" vertical-lob pass. A second exception was previously mentioned: If trapped, you may take the trap low and then jump high to throw over the top of it.

29. AVOID PROBING THE BASELINE WITH THE DRIBBLE.

This is a danger zone, especially against physical, aggressive teams. You now bring the sixth defender into play and may get pushed out of bounds. The dump off into the middle no-look pass is often stolen at the varsity level because defenses help down and sink immediately as you drive. (Good defensive teams react to the ball, and defenders will leave their assignments and move into a helping position.) Beware of that. If you are a smaller guard and probe the baseline, race through, if possible, with your head up, and be prepared to race to the other side, for if you pick up the ball up in that area, you will find yourself in a really tough spot. I like to use the baseline by passing to a player who is in the lacrosse position with his butt to the baseline and seeing the defense from that perspective. NY hall-of-fame coach Lou DeMello teaches *repeat action*: When you drive baseline and get cut off by a defender, stop your drive just outside the lane and take two dribbles away, lulling the defense while keeping your dribble alive. Then storm right back on your drive to the basket. This is a very effective move, as the weak-side defense will relax, along with the on-ball defender.

30. TRUST YOUR EYES, NOT YOUR DESIRES.

Don't play basketball by predetermining what you are going to do, because the defense will always have an important say on what you should choose as a course of action. Don't predetermine your actions or convince yourself that some opportunity has presented itself if your eyes tell you differently. I recently coached one substitute player who had some brilliant moments but negated those plays by putting his head down and driving into traffic, only to give away possession. Basketball demands that players make decisions and react to the events occurring around them. I may desire to lob the ball to my center for an easy score, but my eyes see a weakside defensive guard lurking for a steal. The eyes don't lie. Don't throw the pass.

31. THROW TWO-HANDED PASSES.

If your hands are like Lebron James and you can palm the ball with one hand, then you may throw one-handed passes, but if not,

DO NOT THROW A ONE-HANDED PASS. What appears to be open at first glance can change quickly, resulting in a turnover when the passer has made a one-handed pass.

Coaching Exceptions:

A one-handed pass off the dribble gets to the open player more efficiently without the defense being quite as ready. This pass is to be taught to the *highly skilled point guard.* Another exception: Off the pick-and-pop as the guard digs into the lane, the *one-handed hook pass* over the shoulder back to your teammate is an effective pass. This pass has to be drilled in practice.

TAKING A FULL TIMEOUT HERE: COACHING PROFILE OF TWO NYCHSAA LEGENDS

Jack Curran was a great influence on my early coaching career and helped me get my first varsity coaching position with just one phone call to the athletic director of New Paltz High School. I began working his summer camp each summer as a 20-year-old. His 55-year dedication to coaching high school baseball and basketball will never be matched.

COACH JACK CURRAN

I first knew Coach Curran as a basketball coach, unaware that he was an equally accomplished baseball coach. He lived in Rye, New York, and commuted to Queens, where he dedicated his life to leading young men through the sports of baseball and basketball. By the time he passed away in March, 2013, at the age of 82, he had won more than 2,600 interscholastic games in baseball and basketball in the extremely competitive AA (the highest division) level of the NYCHSAA. 2,600 victories—not a typo. He coached four NBA players in Kevin Joyce, Brian Winters, Kenny Smith, and Kenny Anderson. Curran was named CHSAA Coach of the Year 25 times in baseball and 22 times in basketball. He also coached Jim Larrañaga, who just led Miami University to the Final 4 in 2023, and even more remarkably led George Mason University to the Final 4 in 2006. Overall, Curran's record was 972–437 as a basketball coach and 1708–523 as a baseball coach. The NYC high school basketball played from the 1950s through 2000 was the very best in the county. Curran was at the top of the mountain throughout all those glory years of New York basketball at its finest.

My first time working the Jack Curran Basketball Camp was in the summer of 1985 at Trenton College in Newark, NJ. I was so unprepared for coaching life at a camp, I didn't even bring sheets for the dorm. I slept in sweatpants and arranged clothes as a sheet. An eighth-grade phenom was tearing people up and had been moved up to the varsity ranks of the camp. His name was Kenny Anderson, a most gifted lefty–ball handler with a court vision like no other. Kenny signed a letter of intent to be a Georgia Tech Yellow Jacket in 1988. As a high school freshman, Kenny would lead Archbishop Molloy to a CHSAA city championship and in that game make a one-handed, snap look-off pass from half-court to the rim with a flair and precision few could ever manage.

The camp returned to its normal home at Fordham University in the summer of 1986. Jack and Gene Doris, the head coach at Archbishop Stepinac and the future athletic director at Fairfield University, ran the camp. I was the 23-year-old coach who was beyond excited to be sitting in a circle of chairs that included Tom Konchalski, Gene Doris, and Jack Curran.

The way Gene Doris got to know me is embarrassing, but he never gave me a hard time about it. A couple of years earlier, I had brought a stacked eighth-grade travel team from Port Chester, and we were on our way to winning the Stepinac CYO tournament before being challenged by a rival coach about the age of my center, Rufus Johnson. He was a 16-year-old eighth grader! I did not realize it, because he was skinny as a dangling string. To make matters even worse, there had even been another incident with my team a day earlier. One of our players found his way into the Stepinac weight room and was adjusting the Nautilus plates before he fell and broke his finger. Gene handled it with great ease, but I was shook. Gene may have liked what he saw of me as a CYO coach, for whenever I needed a reference for my early head-coaching jobs, Gene always had my back.

In my early years of coaching, I made it a point to visit a few of Coach Curran's practices. At one practice, I saw Kenny Smith (TNT Kenny Smith) completing fundamentals such as reverse Mikans and box drills, where one player rolls the ball out and then completes a move versus a defender. For all the wisdom I desired to soak in from Coach Curran, I have never been able to mimic his in-game conduct of sitting calmly like an accountant checking over a ledger of entries. Oh, I have tried! But then again, when you coach in the suburbs, you sometimes have to light more fires under your players.

THE GLIDER

For over 40 years, Tom Konchalski was the best-known talent evaluator of boys' high school basketball players with his *High School Basketball Illustrated*. This report was printed on his typewriter and mailed to colleges who paid Tom a subscription fee. I can imagine him now, handwriting an address on each envelope and going to the post office, in contrast to how easily this could be done by email, today. Tom traveled throughout the NY metro area evaluating the best high school players in New York, New Jersey, and Connecticut.

One important fact: *he did not drive.* When Tom needed to evaluate a guard named Frenchy Tomlin at Harding High School in Bridgeport, CT, I was honored to be the driver—although I'm not sure Tom made the best of decisions, given the car I drove in 1986. To this day, my Port Chester friends put me at the top of their list of worst drivers. Tom would have his yellow pad out and be making notes, and I would get to pick his brain. He ranked players from one to five, with five being the highest score one could receive. I finally asked Tom just as a game was about to start, "Tom, what exactly are you looking for in a point guard? What separates the special guards in your mind?" (The answer is given in number 75.)

Frenchy Tomlin would eventually play for Cleveland State, and to this day I don't know what number Tom assigned to him in his evaluation. Chris Mullin, Jamal Mashburn, Pearl Washington, Marc Jackson, Bernard King, and all the legends knew the Glider, for he did an evaluation on each. When Tom was in his last days, Coach Holford visited him in the hospital and read Tom's detailed description of a rising eighth-grade CYO player; the evaluation went on for pages. The name of the eighth grader: Lew Alcindor (Kareem Abdul-Jabbar).

Tom never had a family of his own. This tall, lanky, kind, and gentle graduate of Archbishop Molloy High School had a calling—a mission—and his mission was to prevent worthy players from getting overlooked. He helped over a thousand players (easily) find basketball matches at colleges and universities at all levels of the NCAA. I remember him telling me about a tough guard he liked from a Catholic school in Staten Island and this discovery by Tom may have helped him land a Division II scholarship to play for Charlie Marquardt at Molloy College in Queens. The Jamal Mashburns of the basketball world didn't need Tom, but many players who graduated to DIII and DII schools credit him for giving them the stamp of approval.

What was most special about Tom was the feeling of love and kindness that emanated from the simple gesture of a handshake, which he gave to most everyone. A handshake. He would grab your hand with two of his, look you square in the eyes and ask in a caring voice, "How are you? I have not seen you for a few years. I understand you are coaching at Putnam Valley." He possessed a sincerity few ever match.

Tom passed away in hospice care in the Bronx on February 8, 2021, at the age of 74, from prostate cancer. The NYCHSAA has marched on with love and remembrance for their loyal son and a hole that will never be filled. But the NYCHSAA community was uplifted with great news this past year, when Tom Konchalski was named to the 2023 Class of the Naismith Memorial Basketball Hall of Fame.

Shooting the Basketball

32. SHOOT THE BASKETBALL.

A good shooter cures a lot of ailments. Put the time and effort in to become a better shooter. You may not be graced with the talent to dunk the basketball, but anyone can improve at shooting. Good shooters obviously improve their team's chances of winning by putting points on the board, but they also do something more: they make the defense spread out, thus opening up post play and opportunities to drive to the basket. Good shooting begins with mechanics and repetition, and finishes with the mental muscle of confidence. So get going. Practice more. Shoot more.

Coaching Exemplar:

Rick Pitino was the first college coach to utilize the three-point shot in college ball at Providence, taking the team to the Final 4 in 1987. Pitino would cite the mathematical truism that 33 percent from the three-point line is 50 percent for inside the three. He would reinforce this, stating that making four baskets out of twelve shots from the three-point line results in the same number of points as shooting six for twelve from inside the three. Pitino's embrace of the three and Providence's Final 4 appearance were harbingers of today's three-point-centric NBA.

Coaching Bonus Tip:

Shooting off the catch begins with shot preparation prior to receiving the basketball. Now, what exactly are sound shot-prep fundamentals? You should be ready with your feet under you, knees slightly bent, and your hands providing a clear target. If you are receiving the pass from the inside-out then you need to 1-2 step into the shot (right-handed shooters will step left, right, and then shoot). When shooting off the dribble, sound fundamentals include having a low, hard dribble and bent knees, to go from low to high into your shot.

33. DEVELOP PROPER MECHANICS OF SHOOTING.

Work on that shot! I take pride in teaching shooting because it is *the essential* offensive skill. You want to improve your mechanics and then get in lots of reps. Stephen Curry stepped away from the AAU circuit around eighth grade and his father, a former sharp-shooting NBA pro, spent time deconstructing and then reconstructing his shooting form. Mechanics. Here are some the areas I focus on. Try some of them:

1. Take elbow-in, one-handed shots from just in front of the basket. We move back a step after every two shots made in a row until we make one-handed shots from the foul line, for a total of ten makes, if there are no misses.

2. The ball sits on the finger pads, which are the ends of your fingers.

3. The ball *does not sit in the palm,* but rather there is a gap you can slide two fingers under.

4. Put your shooting pointer finger on the valve and offset three fingers to the side with your thumb at ten o'clock for a righty (two o'clock for a lefty).

5. Stand with your feet shoulder-width apart, facing the rim. A string placed at your big toe and extended to the basket should run to the middle of the rim.

6. Your guide hand is *so critical.* Too many players get side spin on their shots because of poor placement. Some shooters literally block their own shots because of their improper guide-hand placement. Place the tips of three fingers on the side of the ball, very lightly. You are really a one-handed shooter with a guide hand that provides balance and support.

7. Loading position: For younger players, it is just fine to load lower than where a varsity player would load, because of a lack of strength. High school players: let your arm hang at the side of the body and gently swing it back and forth

until you form the shooting L above your shoulder. That position should end for a righty loading up about eyebrow height off the right shoulder (lefty off the left shoulder), but *you won't block your vision* because the ball is loaded off your shoulder, not in the middle of your body. The follow-through expectations are the same. Finish high and snap the wrist with your fingers pointing to the target.

8. Arc is important. Don't have a flat arc. Be wary of insane moon ball arcs—but I have seen very high-arc shooters be successful. I have not seen flat shooters succeed. Use your legs (a quick, short knee bend) and arc to get the ball to the target.

9. Your weight should be on the balls of your feet, and after a three you should land on balance in the same place where you left the floor, or slightly forward.

10. Aim for the imaginary funnel above the rim. Find the middle of three net hooks. Sometimes the center of the rim is in between two hooks. There is a perfect center point of the rim, no matter where you stand, be it baseline, wing, or top.

34. IS THAT SHOT OF YOURS A RUNNER OR A HOPE AND PRAYER?

The runner shot was not so popular when I first started coaching. At Rye, we told players to be on balance, and to shoot and land in the same place, or a half-step forward. The runner became a useful tool for smaller players, as they got by their man, conscious of attempts to block from behind. Steve Nash and Tony Parker, two NBA greats who dominated the early 2000s, were just two NBA players who used the move quite often. Steve Nash was superb at coming off a ball screen and digging into the elbow for one-legged runner shots off the dribble, without stopping and allowing the defender to catch up. Now it seems that every point guard in the NBA has a runner in his arsenal.

I love Jalen Brunson's floaters and of course those of the electrifying Ja Morant. It is a great shot to have in the arsenal. But for most middle school and high school players (boys and girls) it is too often *a hope-and-prayer shot.* Too many players begin their move head down and get caught going too fast without a plan. The result of no plan and trying to salvage an out-of-control drive is to heave up a hope-and-prayer runner. What's the solution? If you are going to shoot runners, try making 25 on the side at each practice. Choose the shot with this thought in mind: If I can get this shot off by stopping and popping and it won't get blocked, then why shoot a runner? Shot fake, one dribble go by, and pull up.

Simply, the runner is needed against a defender who is harder to shake and more attached to your hip. If you don't have the balance and jumping ability needed for a runner, then try to draw a foul with a very hard shot fake and by cutting off the angle of the recovering defender. A final option is to pass and then get the ball right back if needed, or pass and cut through. Did you just shoot a runner, or was that a hope and prayer?

35. SIGHT THEN SHOOT. NEVER SHOOT THEN SIGHT.

This is a problem primarily, but not solely, related to post play. As a player is releasing his shot, I can often tell that it is almost destined for failure. How do I know? The player has not even sighted the target. Quick-turnaround, challenged, inside shots account for most of these "hope-for-the-best" shots. The player may fear being blocked and thus rush the shot attempt, but in that rush, something very critical to a shot's success—or lack thereof—occurs. The target, the rim, has never been identified by the shooter. The shooter is trying to rely on the feel and guesswork of the distance involved and believes he can get that ball in the hole if it isn't blocked. These rushed shots rarely go in the basket. Slow down. Use a strong up fake, and as the defender is on the way down, you as the offensive player can then go up. *Make sure you see your target.* Post players are not alone in risking a hope for the best. At times, wings drive and shoot off the dribble, but because of poor technique (the lack of a hard dribble and a slow transition taking the ball to the shooting pocket), the player focuses so much on the process that the target gets lost. Sight. Shoot. Sight. Shoot. *Never shoot then sight.*

36. HUNTING SHOTS AND "MY-TURN" SHOTS.

The game takes certain ebbs and flows. Sometimes you may feel like you need to score because you aren't in the flow and may not have seen the ball much in the previous few possessions. Do not force a *my-turn shot.* Make the *one more,* and pass up a good shot for a better shot. Taking a tough, challenged shot is as good as a turnover. A bad shot is as good as a turnover. On the flip side, *a team's scorer needs a hunt-the-shot mentality and a desire for the ball in crunch time.* As coaches we need to put our best players in situations where we get them the ball and play through those players. In some years, you may only have one reliable scorer. In this case, the excellent scorer has an increased responsibility to shoot, drive for himself, or draw extra defenders and kick to an open teammate.

Don't shoot versus hunt the shot may seem like a paradox or confusing message, so let's review. Average and below-average scorers should not take my-turn shots, but a scorer has to have a hunt-the-shot mentality. The scorer needs to work hard to get open and catch with a gunslinger mentality, ready to shoot if there is no contest. Even a scorer needs to respect the game and play smart.

37. BAD SHOOTERS ARE ALWAYS OPEN.

If you are consistently open with the ball in your hands, you may not want to hear the reason. Pete Carril, the legendary Princeton coach said it best: "Bad shooters are always open." Coaches scout. Even without scouting, players on the floor quickly realize when a player is a weak shooter. They know if you can't shoot, and they'll leave you open. Maybe you are good at 15 feet and in but have talked yourself into thinking you are better from the three-point line. Know your strengths and weaknesses. Bad shooters can help their teams in numerous ways. Defend. Communicate on the floor. Rebound. Set screens.

38. CHOOSE THE OPEN 12-FOOTER OVER THE CHALLENGED 4-FOOTER.

Take the open shot over a challenged shot. For example, you fill the lane on a three-against-two fast break and receive the ball for an open shot from twelve feet, and yet you decide to pass up that shot, drive closer, and try to score from four feet out—and run smack into a defender. Pros even make this mistake. In his first round 2023 playoff game against the Cavaliers, RJ Barret forced the action in a three-on-two break that lacked spacing, and forced a driving-challenged shot. Pull up from 14 feet and bang the shot. Later in the game, Julius Randle dropped a lead pass because he was ready to drive into traffic. Not good. Why does it happen so often? The player does not *catch and sight rim*. If the player sights the rim, he may notice that he is open for a shot, and he can better read the defenders he is about to confront if he drives. If you are even a decent free-throw shooter, you should shoot around 70 percent. I assure you that you are not shooting anywhere near 70 percent on a challenged shot. You may also charge, and that can get you put on the bench for fouls. If you catch and jump stop under control, you not only have an open shot, but a defender may also leave the basket area to close on you, leaving a teammate wide open under the basket.

39. DIP FOR THREE-POINT SHOTS.

Dipping a ball is when you drop the ball down below your waist to gather momentum for your shot prior to loading the ball back into your shooting pocket. It is a technique that should *not* be used *inside* the three-point line, unless a player can't reach the basket without it.

Years ago, coaches were told *not to allow players to dip*. I coached Ryan Basso, an excellent shooter at Putnam Valley High School, NY, from 2013 through 2015. He scored 50 points in a game once, knocking down three-point shots, seemingly from everywhere— and to think that I was almost considering tinkering with his shot! He had great fluidity and a kinetic chain of energy through his quick dip. The best three-point shooters in the NBA dip. The quick drop of the ball toward the waist as the shooter bends to get power from the lower half of the body and then the fluid reload into the shot is utilized by almost all NBA three-point shooters.

40. FINISH.

Coaches, get on your players who don't consistently finish in practice and in games. This isn't horseshoes; close doesn't count. Concentrate. Use the backboard five feet and in. Coaches can assist in this by not only emphasizing finishing, but by working on finishing moves. Coach Kelly would always remind players at Rye High School that "good players finish." At Gauchos practices, we usually worked on finishing moves for half of the time. Everyone had a ball, and players waiting in line as we ran two lines simultaneously were not allowed to stop dribbling. Practice making finishing moves at game speed. Practice the various types of layups, such as the traditional one-handed layup off one leg and the two-footed power layup off two feet (a pump fake can also be added). Reverse layup finishes are a necessary tool in the arsenal. High school players may add an inside-hand layup. Another finishing move off drives from the middle of the key into the paint is to jump stop, pivot off the foot closer to the sideline, and go up and under as you fake a fadeaway. Then, of course, there are all the dribbling moves to practice into the final, finishing layup. They include crossover, through the legs, behind the back, and inside-out moves. NYC players *get to the cup.* Jim Kelly's constant reminder at Rye High School continues to echo: Good players finish.

Corpus Christi Cougars—5th and 6th grade CYO, 1979–80. I am 17 years old, coaching my brother Dan, 10 years of age, in the front row wearing #22, third one from the left. In that same gym on Friday nights, I became a disco skating security guard. No wonder Coach Kelly could never figure us Port Chester guys out.

Front row, left to right: Charlie Rosabella, Frank Sileo, Dan McDonnell, Steve Devico; *Back row, left to right:* Billy Gargone, Chris Carriero, Steven Rosabella, Anthony Zac, John Goodliffe, Lou Salfi. I am standing next to Coach John Stracuzzi in the very back.

1990–1991 Horace Greeley Varsity team. Bottom row, *left to right:* Nico Karagosian; Ken Rosenblatt; Drew Margolis; Ryan Farrell; Josh Block; Tom Celiberti. Top row, *left to right:* Sean Locke, Warren Simon, Judd Henry, Greg Martin, Coach McDonnell, Alex Hillel, Duncan Burns, David Goldshore, Tom Burns

My greatest recruiting job ever! Me with Debbie Kachmar, before she became my wife.

My wife and me with our girls in Annapolis, Maryland. God blessed me with girls, and it provided balance in my life after coaching boys.

Coach Chris DiCintio and I celebrated the winning of the gold medal at the New York State Empire State Summer Games: College Division. *Players left to right:* Jason Holmes, Desmond Q. Jones, Ryan Schneider, Ryan Stilphon, Jason Boone, Matt Hickey.

Enjoying the 2006 New York State Summer Empire Games with my three daughters: Jillian, Jenna, and Jolie.

Sacred Heart boys win the annual John Volpe Holiday Tournament, with the New York State coaching legend holding the trophy. Coach Steve Marcellino is on the far left. I am on the far right, with Coach Tom Brown next to me.

Left to right: Jelani Bell Isaac, Zachary Coleman, Zach Nolan, me, James Fitzgerald, Ryan Basso. My first starting five at Putnam Valley. League champs/Sectional finalist.

Timeout Putnam Valley: Box Out!

Michael Dutra, my longest serving assistant coach. "Coaches, get yourselves dedicated and talented assistants."

Cutting down the Putnam Valley home court net as we advanced to the Westchester County Center for the fourth time in a five-year span.

Always "Win the Day." Putnam Valley boys in action, with Kevin Gallagher Jr. challenging a shot and Charlie Pagani and Harison Deegan teaming up for a strong box-out down low. Darnel Shillingford in the ready help position in the left corner.

Four-year varsity warrior Darnel Shillingford's 1,000th point.

Photo courtesy of Putnam County News & Recorder

Coach Mac (me) with most of my former Putnam Valley players. Talented, smart, committed, tough ballers!

Timeout Putnam Valley. This is a group I joyously shared three years with, since five of them started as sophomores. So blessed.

Kendahl Kelly, Coach Jim Kelly, Mathias Kelly, and me, in the summer of 2018. I traveled to Svendborg, Denmark, and ran a few basketball clinics at the professional club, the Svendborg Rabbits.

Great group of Kennedy Catholic boys delivered my 300th win, and we overcame the Covid requirements of mask wearing.

Postgame celebration of our 300th victory with staff and my longtime coaching friend, Chris DiCintio, in Somers, New York. Coaches, *left to right:* Jonas Solano, Xavier Lloyd, Owen Lloyd, me, Chris Dicintio.

Me and Coach Robert Holford in the summer of 2023 at the Gauchos Center, almost 25 years after our original collaboration together in the summers of 2000, 2001, and 2002.

My brother, Dan McDonnell, and I posing with my two nephews and two of my daughters. Dan and I are in front; Back row, *left to right:* The cousins: Jolie, Jake, Justin, and Jillian McDonnell.

Summer 2023 with my new girls' basketball program at Briarcliff High School, Briarcliff, New York. *Left to right:* Gemma Fante, Ava Makaron, Adrianna Scanga, and me.

DEFENSE

41. STANCE AND MECHANICS OF ON-BALL DEFENSE.

Guard your yard. Don't give up straight line drives to the basket. Your feet should be shoulder width apart, or slightly wider, with your shoulders over your knees and your weight on the balls of your feet, elbow in, palm facing the shooter above shoulder height, ready to extend and challenge any shot. The offhand (that is, your defending hand facing the offensive player's hand that does not have the ball) is out wide, ready to challenge passes in the passing lane. If the offensive player moves the ball from the right hand to the left hand, you have your right elbow tucked in and palm tracing with your left arm out wide and in the passing lane. Some defenders take one stride off and place their palm in the face of the ball handler. This is a different but effective technique, for it reminds you to be one stride off. Picking up the ball with your feet above the three-point line is far enough for many defenders. Thirty or more feet from the basket, don't cover someone faster than you too closely, or move further from the basket only to get beat.

42. STEALS, FLICKS, DEFLECTIONS, AND CHALLENGED SHOTS.

Be active on defense: active hands, active feet. Sprint to get ahead of the ball. Hustle on closeouts to challenge shots. We must get *flicks from behind* and deflections in the half-court and on presses. For an active-hands reminder, get your hands stretched wide and away from your chest and shoulders with thumbs pointing to shoulders. *Thumbs to shoulders.* As for steals, I remind players that a sin of commission is often better than a sin of omission, so be aggressive and make some plays.

Coaching Bonus Tip:

Flick up when trying to dislodge the ball from behind. Referees call fouls when you swipe downward. Always swipe up. *Always swipe up.* When you block the ball, try to block up and away. If you make the cleanest of blocks with a rapid movement down, don't be surprised to hear the officials whistle.

43. CHARGES IN THE AGE OF THE EUROSTEP.

If a player is coming full speed at one of our defenders, we are aware that the charge may leave the player defending air as the player Eurosteps past. Wall up with hands straight up, as if you are screwing light bulbs in the ceiling, and challenge the shot, jumping as high as you can. Own your space from the floor to the ceiling. If the player is a larger player lacking side-to-side mobility, a traditional charge attempt may be the better choice. *DON'T DO NEITHER*. Either jump high and challenge as best you can, making it clear to the refs that your hands are straight up, or take a charge.

Player Bonus Tips:

Most charges occur helping off a player and stepping early enough into the driver's path. (Helping off means leaving your assigned defender to stop the ball handler.) Another charge opportunity is to fight so hard to get over a ball screen that you force the screener to set a moving screen. A good defender should sell that foul (acting class 101) a bit and go flying. The Miami Heat excel at this. Finally, if you move your feet and take proper angles with your on-ball defense, you can draw the charge against the person you are defending.

44. BLOCK WITH THE INSIDE HAND, STRIP THE BALL, OR CLEAN, HARD FOUL: THREE WAYS TO RECOVER.

If the player is a stride or two ahead of you, racing to the basket ahead of the field, think of these three options. First, you may block with your inside hand if you are tall enough or jump high enough to make it happen. Tuck your stomach in and block without contact. If you choose the wrong hand to block, then your body will come across and cause contact. You block a left-hand layup with your right hand and vice versa. If you don't see the block as a viable option, but can get to a hard run by stripping off the ball with fast hands before the opponent rises for the layup, this is often a great option. If the ball is protected by the offensive player, a final option is the *clean, hard foul across the arms.* We never, ever get under our opponent's feet and legs. We do not ever want to cause an injury to our opponent, especially a lower body injury. Do not give up a soft and-one foul resulting in a three-point play. No soft and-ones. Ever.

45. FIGHT TO GET THROUGH SCREENS AND/OR AVOID SCREENS ALTOGETHER.

Bad defenders are always screened. Good defenders know how to both fight through screens and avoid them altogether. Bad defenders walk smack into screens, often appearing to be hugging a friend. Here are a few tips to get through and around screens: Keep your arms and hands away from your body so that screeners don't get into your chest. Defending against double and triple screens along the baseline, you need to go *outside hip,* which means you may have half your body out of bounds, and you sprint to close the deal on the catch. If you are in a zone and on the weak side, *DO NOT TURN YOUR ENTIRE BODY TO THE SIDELINE AND BALL WATCH.* Instead, have your butt facing the baseline and *use pistols with your two hands.* One hand points like a gun to the ball and the other to an offensive player on the weak side (pistols-out stance). Swivel your head back and forth, ready to fight over any flair screen. In man-to-man, off a down screen on the wing, your teammate should give you a lane to step through or pull you through. On a ball screen, if your coach asks you to fight over the top and provides a forward to hedge for you, you need to skinny up and get over. *Skinny up* is fancy talk for don't have your butt sticking out and run dead smack into the screen.

Coach Robert Holford Getting Screened Anecdote:

Once, at a practice at Eugenio María de Hostos Community College in the Bronx, a player did not get through a double-stagger screen along the baseline, even though Coach Holford had taught his team to avoid the screen by using the outside-hip technique. Get ready for what I'm about to tell you: With his arm extended, Coach Holford sprinted at three-quarter speed through the two defenders—like a construction-site wrecking ball—and loudly proclaimed: "You take the screeners out!" I'm not saying that this is a sportsman-like move, but it is important to realize how detrimental getting screened is to your defense. Remember: *Bad defenders are always screened.*

46. IN ZONE, FIND A MATCHUP,
BECAUSE THE WOOD HAS NEVER SCORED.

When playing zone defense, be sure to find a player in your area to matchup and defend. Very good offensive teams move the ball and the players to create confusion, especially with the reward of three-point shooting. Some teams don't even post anyone up against a zone, and their approach is to create three-versus-two and two-versus-one situations because some player has doubled down to the high post when not needed or covered the wood down in the paint and the offense has put all five players from the middle to one side. The wood has never scored. Find someone to be your matchup. This even means in a 2-3 zone that a bottom forward on a zone may have to go across to cover a player 10 to 12 feet out on the other side along the baseline. No use guarding the wood. *The wood has never scored.*

47. GUARD THE WOOD ON
BASKET-OUT-OF-BOUNDS PLAYS.

Make up your mind coach Mac! You just told me not to cover the wood. Well, there is one exception. When you are zone defending a basket out of bounds (BOB), do not leave your forward or center area in the bottom of the 2-3 zone. BOB zone, inbound plays are often designed to *create a vacuum* and then *fill that vacuum*. If you start to follow a low post player away from the basket, that will leave your team very vulnerable to a "pick the picker" or other offensive ploy. As you leave your area following one player, some other offensive player will quickly fill the vacuum you created. Both guards may scramble to cover, but not the forwards.

48. JUMP TWO STEPS TO THE BALL
AFTER EVERY PASS.

No face cuts. A player at the top of the key passes to the left wing, does a fake step to her right, and beats the defender on a cut left to the basket, only to receive the ball back and score a layup! Do not allow a give-and-go pass to be completed. That is the oldest offensive action in basketball. Good defenders do not fall prey to successful passes and cuts through one course of action: Jump two steps toward the ball after the person you are covering has passed it. Let that person go to the opposite side of the court. Immediately after you realize that there is no cut, start to move closer to your assignment, stopping at the midline (in line with the rim) or getting closer if you are guarding an excellent shooter.

Coaching Bonus Tip:

A good drill for this is to play three on three and demand that players continually pass and cut. Stop play anytime you see a defender get face cut.

49. JAM ANY FLASHES TOWARD THE BALL.

The ball is on the left-wing, foul line extended. You are in a helping position (your right foot touches the lane on the opposite side) pointing to your defensive assignment, who is two steps off the lane on the weak side. As the offensive player *flashes* (cuts) to the ball-side elbow, you need to get between the flasher and the

55

ball. You quickly use your left forearm, which is chest high, and bang it into the chest/shoulder of the cutter, beating the cutter to the spot and denying or discouraging the pass with your right hand extended, thumb facing down. If the opponent outweighs you by a lot, you need to sit entirely on top of the cut, because that player may just knock right through your arm.

50. THOU SHALT NOT ENTER THY LANE.

Sounds biblical. If basketball were a religion, this would be a wise and highly valued commandment. Don't get posted up deep. If a post gets real deep, step off and around the post player and sit on top. Be physical with the lower half of your body, but show your hands high to the referees, reinforcing to them that you are not fouling. If an opponent cuts through the paint or lane, make sure they get bumped. A defender may step in their path. A light forearm bump may ensue. Make it clear that you and your teammates own the paint.

Coaching Bonus Tip:

I often remind players that although football is a *collision* sport, basketball is a *contact* sport. So get physical.

51. ON THE LINE. . . UP THE LINE. . . IN THE PRESS.

You are in a man press and covering a player at half-court. He suddenly bursts toward the ball, and you get beat, allowing him to easily catch the inbounds. Now, let's do this better. Begin one big stride closer to the ball than the offensive player. If the player breaks long, you sprint and close the gap while the ball is in the air like an NFL cornerback. If the player you are covering now begins at the foul line in the backcourt at the foul line extended, you start a half stride behind so you don't get beat long. Close the gap if the player flashes toward the ball. If he receives the ball off the inbounds, jump one stride off immediately, ready to make the ball handler work to get up the court. This one-stride spacing keeps you from picking up a quick foul and from getting immediately beat.

52. FAN OUT AND LOCATE SHOOTERS IN DEFENSIVE TRANSITION.

It is not enough to just get back and hustle into the paint. The defenders must immediately fan out and locate the shooters, especially late trailers looking for a kick out. With the prevalence of the three-point shot in today's game, you must get back and make sure you find that potential three-point threat.

53. CHALLENGE THE SHOOTING SLOT.

How should you exactly challenge a shot? Should your hand be in the eyes of the shooter or up high in line with the shooting pocket? Challenge the shooting slot. Do not foul the shooter. Do not get into the shooter's landing area. Hopefully, the official will not reward an awkward attempt by the shooter to kick the leg out and draw contact, but sometimes a shooter will get away with that illegal maneuver. On a closeout, sprint and break down into short, choppy steps. Bad closeouts result in shot-fake drives. If there is a shooter on the scouting report, and we are forced to get there late because of rotations, just do a hard one-handed *run-by* challenge. With a strong defending, rebounding team that runs by, a closing defender can release for the fast break.

Shooting contested shots results in a dramatic decline in offensive efficiency, so closeouts are imperative. Your coach may not allow you to help off a ball-side drive, thus leaving the corner three-point shot open. That coach may want you to stunt and stay. Other coaches will teach that the ball scores and demand that you leave your assignment and stop the ball. Regardless, take pride in closing out (two strides, sprint, and short, choppy finishing steps).

54. TAKE AWAY THE OPPONENT'S BEST SCORER WITH LOCK DENIALS AND LOCK SHADES.

When you are assigned to be a *lock defender* against the other team's best scorer, you have *no help responsibilities*. Your one mission is to make it extremely difficult on the scorer. Deny your person the ball, and stop the scorer from getting easy baskets. If you are ball screened, your coach should demand a trap of the ball with you holding active hands high and your teammate, who was covering the screener, joining you in that trap. Against good passers and more experienced players, coaches will often trap just to get the ball out of the star scorer's hands and get back to their assignments, rather than risk a pass for an easy score. Even when you are the lock defender, your entire team should be helping you, not placing the onus on you alone. Remember: box out. Don't give up easy offensive rebound put backs, and don't commit needless fouls.

Bonus Coaching Tip:

Go to a *lock shade* instead of straight lock when the opposing scorer is a very quick wing or point. By close shading and not all-out denying, the defender is less apt to get beat on a back cut. All other rules of *no help* still apply.

55. DEFENDING THE TWO ON ONE.

The defender needs to sprint ahead to the lane and then hard jab and drop. As Coach Holford would often say, "Guard the cage." I always tell players a jump shot is on us (the coaches), but a layup is going to count against you. No soft and-one fouls leading to three-point plays. If you force the jump shot, we may get a second defender back in the play. A speeding guard may be a prime target for a charge. Step up quickly and take that charge as your opponent tries to throw the ball ahead.

56. USE THE I-FORMATION DEFENDING
THE THREE-ON-TWO FAST BREAK.

Get in an I-formation. Meet the ball in the key area, ready to jump outside the three-point line to challenge. If the guard pulls up from 23 feet and splashes a three, that is acceptable. Remember, we are in an outnumbered situation to begin with, so we are playing the odds. The back of the tandem goes to the shooter and the top drops. If the ball is swung back to the top, we *do not charge back out* with the defender who has dropped. That defender protects the cage. The defender who covers the first pass scrambles to the second pass up top. Hopefully, our trailers are sprinting back to join in the defensive transition.

Transition

I had an opportunity to work with Coach Mike D'Antoni during the fall of his last season with the New York Knicks. I co-coached an AAU fall team which had Mike's oldest son on the team. Since the next section is *Transition,* this is the perfect place to discuss this fun fall that I enjoyed.

COACH MIKE D'ANTONI, Head NBA Coach, *Denver Nuggets, Phoenix Suns, NY Knicks, Houston Rockets, and Los Angeles Lakers.* **Assistant Coach,** *Gold Medal-Winning US Men's National Basketball Team, 2008 and 2012.*

Coach Mike D'Antoni is coaching the NY Knicks, the fall prior to their getting Carmelo Anthony, and my dear buddy Chris DiCintio is coaching Mike's son, who is a junior at Rye High School. I combine four of my Sacred Heart of Yonkers players with five of Chris's Rye players for a fall AAU team. Chris invites me to co-coach the team with him. I can't believe I am in Eastview, NY, at the Knicks' training center. At the first practice, Mike and his brother, Dan, are running drills. Coach DiCintio stealthily whispers to me that maybe he or I should run a drill or two, so we can show Coach D'Antoni that we can coach too, in order to not look incompetent. I quickly respond, "If two NBA coaches want to run drills, then let them run as many as they want." My point guard, John Gause, the only sophomore I ever named captain, went home to Mount Vernon after that first practice and reported, "I was so excited about the practice I went home and [vomited]."

Well, who could blame him? We not only proceed to practice at the Knicks' facility the entire fall, but we learn the Knicks' offense in their film-viewing room with its spacing and drag-ball screens (which were once utilized masterfully by Steve Nash and Amar'e Stoudemire). You give Mike D'Antoni a point guard, you better look out! We use the Knicks' film room, and Coach D'Antoni breaks down tapes of the Knicks' offense, teaching us the various options. He ends up running practices, and Chris and I coach the games—and I am just fine with that arrangement.

Come game time, Mike sat deep in the bleachers and never once questioned anything we ran. I was already a huge fan of Mike's "Seven Second Offense" from his Phoenix Suns days, and to learn his half-court system was a treat. Mike would go on to great success with James Harden and the Houston Rockets and get another contract with the Lakers. I still remember Chris and me urging Mike to join us on the bench at a gym in Rockland County, but he would always decline—a brilliant basketball mind who may have won an NBA championship, if Chris Paul had not been injured. But as much as I admire him, I think my friend, Chris DiCintio, a most innovative high school matchup zone and press specialist, should run his defense.

57. PLAY THROUGH THE TRAIL
ON THE BREAK / HI-LOW.

Love to fast break. The rim runner is the 4- or 5-man, and his partner trails. Off a made basket, you can have a *permanent, inbounding post player* and a permanent rim runner. Off a miss, the rebounding post player is the trailer, and the other post player is the rim runner. We like to have the trailer yell "TRAIL!" It is the best way to feed the post or go into other actions, such as a reversal and follow the pass ball-screen–pick-and-roll, as we lift the original rim runner to remove the help. Off a made basket, I like to push the ball up the sideline, thus pushing the 2-man (the right wing) toward the corner and then pass to the point close to the sideline, thus leaving much space for the trailer running dead center of the court and being available between midcourt and the top of the key. Defenses run back to the paint, so don't crowd into the trailer's area. On a miss, if the point guard keeps the dribble and is coming up the middle toward the right elbow, then the rebounding post player hustling upcourt should trail two strides behind and communicate loudly: *"TRAIL!"* Off a miss, a great pass for the trailer is a jump stop just inside the foul line, reverse pivot, with a Euro underhand, flip pass. The trailer has the high-low pass, a shot, or ball reversal actions.

58. REBOUND, QUICK OUTLET, START THE BREAK, ESCAPE THE TRAP.

Options. Off a rebound, be ready for the opponent to try to win the ball right back. Snatch the ball firmly with two hands. Turn to the outside—*not* the inside—and look to outlet to your sideline or to the middle (the sideline has the greater chance of being open, though years ago the New Jersey Nets would run a great break-hitting Jason Kidd in the middle of the floor with wings jetting upcourt). If the outlets are denied and you are a good ball handler, start the break yourself with a turn and a very *low* blowout dribble. Keep your head up (sight rim) and be ready to immediately lead pass the ball. Be aware of players behind you. If there are two defenders trying to jam you in the middle of the paint, make an escape with two speed dribbles to the sideline to get away from the trap. With all three of these strategies, remember that you must assume the defense will attempt to win the ball back. Be tough. Be strong with the ball. Act decisively.

Coaching Bonus Tip:

The better you are as a running team, the less likely you are to be pressed. If a team is still hell-bent on jamming the outlet by double teaming and swarming the rebound, punish that strategy with layups, and they will change their approach.

59. PUSH AND PULL TO HANDLE A PRESS.

Wings being pressed and on the outside should be taught to

take the defender up (that is the *push*) to go long and to take the defender long (that is the *pull*) to go up, or shall we say back, toward the inbounder. This is how you get open. Very important to not play flat-footed. Move. Get open.

Coaching Bonus Tip:

I am not crazy about using players at half-court who flash to the ball in a press break, because if the defender is on the line and up the line (cheating a stride ahead of the flash, like a defender should), that defender will have a lot of time to recover. Instead, I like to either position that player further downcourt or more in the backcourt top of the key extended, so that if he *pushes up, the pull-long pass* is easier to execute.

60. DEMAND THE BALL ON A RIM RUN.

When you make a rim run, demand the ball. You are not out there for a track exhibition. The primary objective of the sprint out is to get the ball and score. There are two moves a rim runner can make in order to bury the defender behind him: the arm-over slash and box-out or a reverse spin into the body of the defender and seal with your legs wider than shoulder width and your arms spread wide and high, elbows above shoulders. (To *seal* is to clearly keep the defender behind you, providing an unobstructed passing lane between you and the passer.) If you are rim running and the defender is still with you at half-court, you may slow down and then pick back up to a sprint pace to throw off the defense. Always be hard to guard. A secondary, yet still significantly positive outcome, of a strong rim run is that you may draw wing defenders to cover up for their slower post defender, leading to open wing runners spotting up outside the three-point line.

61. INBOUND IMMEDIATELY AFTER A MADE BASKET.

The moment the ball goes through the net, get that ball inbounded. The 5-to-2 pass from the baseline to half-court, executed as a baseball pass, is the first look. A righty inbounder points his left shoulder to the intended target and stands with feet facing the sideline. Remember, after a made basket, the inbounder can run the baseline. It is critical to the break that we get the ball in less than one second. Point guards need to know how to get open for immediate inbounds. And wings get to half-court. Some teams have a designated inbounder, usually the center or power forward and the other post rim runs. An excellent fast break can oftentimes be your best press break.

62. OFFENSIVE EXECUTION OF THE TWO VERSUS ONE.

If you are the ball handler with the basketball and a post player is your partner on this break, don't give the weaker ball handler (your post partner) the ball too early, for this may result in a travel violation or charge. Positioning is very important: both players should be just one step wider than the width of the lane. If you are too wide, you allow the 1 defender too much time to recover. An athletic driver should go strong to the basket and not pass until the defender is squarely in front. That pass may be delivered in a variety of ways, such as an inside-hand bounce pass, whereby the ball handler slices off to the outside so as to avoid any charge. Another method is a behind-the-back pass or lob. If the ball handler is *not* a strong driver and lacks jumping ability, it is wise to stop at the elbow. Jump stop. Pass fake. Shoot. Be under control. Why shoot a challenged driving shot, if you are not strong at finishing? Play to your strengths.

63. OFFENSIVE EXECUTION OF
THE THREE VERSUS TWO.

With the wings sprinting wide and the ball handler pushing down the middle of the court, the wings can begin a 45-degree cut toward the basket inside the three-point line to about 15 feet from the basket. The point passes either left or right and follows the pass to the ball-side elbow. This is critical because now the dropping top defender is placed in the quandary of either covering the elbow or getting beat to the basket by the weak-side wing who continues from 15 feet out to the rim on the weak side. Avoid the common mistake of leaving a lack of spacing and/or a point guard who gets too deep in the lane, thus allowing two defenders to cover three. Another common mistake is to pass up the open 15-footer on the wing and drive into traffic. For some reason, players believe that an outnumbered situation must result in them getting a layup. Take the clean open shot and look to rebound on the weak side in case it is missed. Do not charge from the middle or wing.

Coaching Bonus Tip:

Some varsity coaches run their wings to the three-point line on a three versus two fast break or teach finishers to run toward the basket and shooters to spot up. Be clear on your communication with your players as to exactly what you prefer.

64. BALL SCREEN AND RESCREEN AT THE TOP OF THE KEY IN TRANSITION.

On the fast break, it is wise to free up the point guard (especially if the point guard is your scorer) with screen-rescreen action at the top of the key while the wings cross through on the baseline and the rim runner steps out to the short corner (the lacrosse position, behind the net). The point tries to turn the corner from right to left, using the on-ball screen. Oftentimes that first attempt is stopped, but with the post sprinting a few strides and providing an immediate second ball screen for the ball handler (now going left to right), the defender is often unable to fight through twice. The screener should roll or pop and stay high for a possible pass back from the point. Some coaches like the one-handed hook pass back to the pop man. This pass is a very good one for the talented, varsity-level guard.

Coaching Bonus Tip:

On the wings, cutting through action (left wing to right side and vice versa), the right wing stops for one second under the net and screens for the left wing coming through. The right screener then continues out to the left wing. The left wing *always* crosses below the right. This prevents them from crashing into each other. This is my favorite secondary break action, for it allows for three-on-three basketball instead of five-on-five. Advantage: offense.

Two Greatest College Coaches of All Time

COACH JOHN WOODEN AND A 1976 RED MONTE CARLO

Coach John Wooden is coming to Newton, MA, for a Nike Medalist Coaching Clinic, and I learn of it just hours before his arrival. John Wooden! The Wizard of Westwood who won 10 national championships in a 12-year period, starting in 1964. I am 18 years old in the spring of 1981, and my dad is away on a trip. He wouldn't know if I took his red-and-white trim, 1976 Monte Carlo up to Boston—would he? Irrelevant. It is better to ask for forgiveness than for permission. My friend John Stracuzzi joins me for the ride, and we somehow get directions. How did we get to places without Waze?

Wooden did not speak about his 2-2-1 press or 2-1-2 half-court high-post offense, but rather he spoke about practice preparation, mental balance, and putting on socks properly. I should have gotten more from his talk than I did, but I was too young to fully appreciate the love he had for *planning his practices* and how he saved every practice plan in a binder. He saved all of his practices from every year of his long and illustrious coaching career. Amazing. A young prep school coach spoke at that clinic, as well. His name was Gary Williams. He would find much success at Boston College and lead Maryland to a national championship in 2002.

When my father came home from his trip, would he notice a change in his total car mileage? Nah. No way. He's a guy. My wife once changed our living room drapes and did not say anything to me, waiting to see if I would notice. One month later, I picked up on the change.

COACH K

Coach Mike Krzyzewski advanced to his first Final 4 in 1986, defeating the David Robinson–led Naval Academy by a score of 71–50. Duke would finish with a 37–3 record that year, losing in the championship game to the University of Louisville 72–69. This was the team Coach K refers to as the bedrock of the great Duke program and all the success that ensued over his more than 40-year tenure there as head coach. The 1982 recruiting class included Johnny Dawkins, David Henderson, Jay Bilas, and Mark Alarie. This was the class Coach K knew that he needed to replicate in 1986, as these four seniors were graduating.

At eleven one morning, Coach Jack Curran asked me, the gofer, if I could pick up Coach Mike Krzyzewski at LaGuardia Airport, for Mike was scheduled to speak at one o'clock at the camp. At the time, he wasn't the household name that he is today, but he had been at Duke since 1980, and he entered the NCAA tourney that year as the one seed. He was a Final 4 coach and in the best college league, the Atlantic Coast Conference (ACC). I was of course looking forward to picking him up. You could tell that Coach K was feeling good and at the top of his game, for he was tanned and in a sharp Duke polo shirt exuding a peace and calm that comes with success. I did not hesitate to let Coach K know that I wanted to be a successful coach and was open to any advice he could give. He gave me an immediate answer about bringing focus, passion, and my best efforts to every game. He was humble, friendly, and talkative throughout the ride, and I took to heart what he said. I treat every game, maybe to a fault—even in the offseason—with passion, focus, and a desire for excellence, remembering Coach K's words.

POST FEEDING AND POST PLAY

65. BEHIND MEANS OPEN, SO FEED THE POST.

Feed the post. Good guards, even in the age of three-point shooting, must be able to feed the post. It does not matter how much a defender mauls the post player if that defender is behind your teammate. Behind means open, and open means that the post player must be fed the ball unless another help defender is lurking nearby. A guard who violates our sight-rim rule will not even realize the post is open and miss the opportunity. A guard who catches and dribbles immediately loses sight of the court. A guard who is looking for his own scoring may ignore the post player. If guards don't feed the post, the posts will stop working to get open. If you play for me and don't feed the post, you become my assistant coach. Grab a chart.

66. SEE THE POST, READ THE POST, FEED THE POST.

Coach Holford preached this all the time. It seems that he got this from Gordon Chiesa, the former assistant coach for the Utah

Jazz. Follow these three steps: After seeing the post, read where the defender is, and *pass away from the defense.* For example, if the post is three-quarter fronting with a hand disrupting the entry pass, lead the offensive player with a pass toward the middle and vice versa, if the situation is reversed where your pass may lead the player toward the basket. Here is a great tip: *a pass one step away from the offense is two steps away from the defense, and the defender simply can't get to two steps, thus making your pass very difficult to steal.* You must also read the *weak-side* defender and make sure that as you lead your teammate away from one player, you are not leading her into another defender or passing the ball away to the opponent.

Lobs:

When you throw a lob, lead a post player toward the direction of the corner of the backboard away from the middle, where there may be more defensive help. The post player positioning for the lob needs to box out and keep contact with the defender until the moment the ball is passing his shoulder. The receiving post player *must keep the ball high* and never drop it low, even for a split second, exposing the ball to rugrats. Those little guards are always lurking for steals. Other post-feeding notes: fake high to throw low and fake low to throw high, and feed the ball past the on-ball defender's ear (who can't get his hand from the low back to his ear in time). Use the hook bowling-ball pass off a high fake.

Feeding the high post versus a zone:

Against zones, we bounce pass or lob to get it into the high post at the foul line area. No chest pass versus a zone to get the ball to the high post.

67. GET LOW AND WIDE IN THE POST.

Elbows out, get low and wide, thumbs to ears (Mickey Mouse ears), demanding the ball. Deep in the low post is not the only good place to post. You are often easier to double on the weak side from there. The NBA 6-to-10-foot post up off the lane can be quite effective. If you are being fronted and the ball is being reversed for a hi-low, *keep your body contact and reverse pivot, calling for the ball to be led away from the defense.* When the coach runs a clear out because he sees a mismatch, do not give up any ground, get low and fight for every inch. Referees will let smaller guards foul post players from the waist down, so don't expect a call against a smaller defender. *Don't feel sorry for a smaller defender.* Bury that defender under the rim.

68. CHIN AND CHECK.

Off a post catch, squeeze the ball with two hands and bring it just under your chin with your elbows out. Check the defense. Scan your surroundings. Are you being double teamed? Maybe you can make your one-on-one move before the double team arrives. You might fake a pass back out to get a potential double-teaming defender to stop in place. You pass to a rim-running, basket-cutting post buddy.

69. PICK-AND-ROLL SCREENER:
GO SHORT ROLL AGAINST A TRAP.

If you set the ball screen and see your point getting swarmed by a double team, don't roll deep to the rack, because your point won't be able to deliver you the ball. Instead, stay close to the ball and be available. If the ball handler is cutting across the top of the key from left to right, then the screener *short rolls* and follows the ball above the foul line. Don't continue a roll all the way to the basket, because the point won't be able to deliver the ball to you.

70. GIVE UP POSITION TO KEEP POSSESSION.

When you are in the post, it is important to meet passes and *not let the defender get around you.* All passes are not perfect. Some are off target or have been deflected, so you must always consider that *it is more important to keep possession than it is to keep position.* Let's say you post four feet from the basket and by meeting the bad pass, you are now six feet from the basket. Nothing wrong with that, as long as we maintain possession. What is a problem? If your feet stay stuck in the mud, and that defender gets around and steals the ball, you will be more at fault than the passer. Once again, *it takes two people to make a turnover,* and you as the receiver are now the more guilty party for not having the energy and making the effort to meet the ball.

71. POST PLAYERS: KEEP THE BALL IN PRIVATE PROPERTY—SOMEBODY IS ALWAYS COMING.

You hear coaches say to post players to always keep the ball high, and that is sound advice, for smaller guards are lurking, waiting for you to bring the ball down. A six-foot-five player becomes four feet five when holding the ball down by the waist. But let's take this advice a step further. Get the ball to private property—not public property, but private property, as Ganon Baker, the accomplished basketball trainer says. Absolutely. Move the ball to an area which might be off your left ear if you sense a defender on your right. Windshield-wipe the ball from one side to the other. Give violent head fakes and secure the ball tightly with two hands. *Assume somebody is always coming to block you,* and learn to have that basketball sixth sense. Do not go up softly, get blocked, and act surprised. This isn't you dominating your classmates at lunchtime. You have competition. Why would the defense allow you free, unimpeded points? Be aware. Be tough. Be explosive.

72. NEVER FADE AWAY FROM THE OPPOSING TEAM'S SHOT BLOCKER.

Pump fake and attack the face of the defender. Go through the defender and initiate contact. Pump fake, go at the defender, and try to get to the foul line. The fadeaway plays into the shot blocker's hands. *Do not fade away.* Another option is to kick the ball out to a teammate if you feel you will get blocked and won't get to the line.

That is preferable to the fadeaway. An inside post fade is not the worst shot for a player who has worked on it, but it is not the shot to be used against the opponent's primary shot blocker.

73. CATCH, KICK IT BACK OUT, AND RE-POST.

If the post player feels he received a post pass in an off-balance position or too far away from the basket, then he should kick it back out and bury the defender (who often relaxes for a second when the ball is passed out), two steps deeper. Now the guard has the responsibility of quickly passing it right back to the post player.

74. POST UP ONE STRIDE OFF THE LANE.

I have always focused on teaching my post players to fight for deep-paint touches, but there is another area where I came to utilize my post players, later in my career. Posting up one or even two steps off the lane makes double teaming from the weak side more difficult; it opens up more drives for perimeter players and allows you to face up against a slower defender and take that defender to the rack. In stations, I have posts working on both deep, low-post position and NBA-style, mid-post position. A final effective area to post is one step off the elbow. Carmelo Anthony made many buckets off that post-up location.

General Guard and Perimeter Play

75. LEARN TOM KONCHALSKI'S
FOUR-POINT GUARD ESSENTIALS.

One evening at Harding High School in Bridgeport, CT, Tom Konchalski taught me the four areas where he judged point guards for their college level and readiness.

1. *Assist-to-turnover ratio.* A three-to-one assist-to-turnover ratio is strong.
2. *Easy baskets.* Can the player create easy baskets for others?
3. *Scoring.* Is the player a scoring threat?
4. *Defending.* Can that player stop the opposing guard?

76. POINT GUARD: SET UP THE PICK-AND-ROLL.

Take your defender below the screen to better use the screen. For the more advanced point guard: try to take your defender one step below the screen (you are one step below the screen, closer to the baseline). For example, as you are going down the right wing (foul line extended), keep your body between the defender and the ball. Now, reverse dribble with the ball in your left hand and then get as tight as you can to the screen, thus running your defender into it as you continue looking to dig in toward the elbow for a pull-up or continuing to drive. Keep your body between the defender and the ball, both during the setup, as you are going down the right side, one step below the foul line extended, and when you move to the middle of the floor using your left hand. Simply, when moving to your right, dribble with your right hand, and when moving to your left, dribble with your left hand. Always keep your off arm pointed down and away from your body to fend off the defender.

Player Bonus Tips:

If there is a forward who hedges out, use a pullback dribble and reattack. Off a switch where you have a big covering you, take two pullback dribbles and then attack the big's top foot (the foot furthest away when you first faced the switch). Dribble split if the hedge defender leaves space. Throw the ball out low—very low—and chase it back.

77. ATTACK CLOSEOUTS.

The closeout defender is often vulnerable to a quick, attacking drive toward the paint. I used to think a shot fake was the strongest go-to move prior to the drive, but came to view this technique differently after coaching Mike D'Antoni's son during an AAU season. He would give a slight neck and head movement upward and immediately attack the basket. The shot fake sometimes gives the out-of-balance closeout defender a chance to recover. The Miami Heat is very good at catching skips on the move, thus already having a head of steam against the closeout defender.

78. POINT GUARDS: USE THE 14-FOOT MARK OR FOUL LINE AREA TO YOUR ADVANTAGE.

If you are a strong finisher who can draw contact and finish in traffic, you should play to that strength when the opportunities present. If you are a point guard who is an efficient game manager, then think about 1-2 stopping around the foul line area while reading the battlefield. *Sight rim:* you may have your own shot. If you can get a step inside the foul line, you may be able to draw the post defender to you, fake the shot, and feed your now open teammate down low. If you are passing to the left side of the floor with a defender directly in front of you, do not pass across your body from right to left, but rather windshield-wipe the ball to your left pocket and step out to that side.

Player Bonus Tip:
Don't get too deep and get caught in the land of the giant oak trees. Stop 14 feet out, not 10 feet out.

79. BE HARD TO GUARD.

Good guards keep defenders off balance. Change speeds. Even if you are very fast, a defender can outrun you, because as the ball handler, you have the slowing down factor of the ball, and the defender does not have that burden. By changing speeds and directions, you keep the ball defender off balance. Coach Mike D'Antoni often talked about how important this is. James Harden changes pace, skips, bounces back, and goes forward, and it shows his awareness of the *hard-to-guard* attacking mindset. Jalen Brunson utilizes *hard-to-guard* tricks that send defenders for a loop. For point guards most especially: *CHOOSE TO BE HARD TO GUARD.*

80. BE A COMPLETE GUARD.

This past year, I constantly reminded one of my guards to be more than just a catch-and-shoot-three guy. He was a fair shooter, not great. If you make four for nine one game, that seems very good, but what about the next game where you may make two for eleven? Now, if you can't drive and get to the foul line or get inside for a few 15-footers, you are totally reliant on one, and only one, aspect of guard play. You also aren't creating shots for others if you can't break the defense down and use your dribble for a teammate. In practice, this player stayed in his comfort zone, and I would chide him to use practice as the opportunity to attempt to improve his area of weakness. I would say, "Have fun. Believe. Drive. Do what you don't yet attempt in games, here in practice."

81. REWARD YOUR POST PLAYERS IN TRANSITION.

To be a truly great running team, you need to have the bigs sprinting the floor with spirit and force. There is no better way to completely dishearten the post players than for you to keep firing threes up most every trip and never feeding the post. Reward those post runs. Show some love. Get some easy, close shots.

82. HOW MANY PITCHES HAVE YOU MASTERED?

Lou DeMello, a NY State High School Hall of Fame coach, is now a basketball trainer in upper Westchester County, NY. Lou coached Felipe López, considered the best player in the US in 1994, at Rice High School in Harlem. (Sadly, the small Catholic school closed.) For the advanced player who wants to excel at ballhandling, DeMello emphasizes the number of moves you have to master out of six go-to moves, much like a pitcher in baseball. He makes it clear that pitchers don't need six pitches, but it is better to have at least three—like a fastball, changeup, and curve—instead of one. If you only have a crossover, then within a short period of time, the defense is ready for that one move.

The six moves are as follows:
1. Crossover
2. Through the Legs
3. Behind the Back
4. Reverse or Spin Dribble
5. Inside Out
6. Escape/Pullback

83. HOLD THE BALL FOR TWO SECONDS, OR CLICK IT.

Against a zone, if your post players are x-cutting and flashing to the ball, don't reverse the ball before they get to your side; otherwise, they are working hard for nothing. As a wing, you need to show patience and allow the posts to get to their desired spots. Wait for two seconds for the posts, unless you can take a shot from the wing or find an opposite skip for a guaranteed open shot. If you are the point, you may want to immediately snap-reverse the ball in a fraction of a second to the other wing—not every time, of course. More times than not, catch and allow those posts to get open.

84. ONE MORE. . . ONE MORE!!
MAKE THE "ONE MORE" PASS.

There is nothing more team centered than having a pretty good open look for a shot and choosing to pass it up and make *one more pass* for a better shot. This choice leads to higher field goal percentage, greater team connectivity, and a spirit of winning over individualism. You may pass up a shot on one offensive possession only to be the recipient of a *one-more pass* on another possession.

85. DRIBBLE WITH STRENGTH AND PACE.

A key fundamental to ballhandling is to dribble the basketball with your fingertips as you snap your wrists and follow through with your hand, like you do for a jump shot. Follow through. Follow through. The height of the dribble is often between the knee and thigh. When you are manipulating the ball through tight traffic, you may dip your body lower and take the ball well below your knees. There is a great advantage to using a Magic Johnson–style strong, pounding dribble, where you push the ball downward with force. With that type of strong dribble, pounding the ball close to your hip, you can better face up to a defender and get by her for pull-ups.

There was a point guard named Conor McGuinness from New City, NY. At five feet nine, Conor would make such great use of his strong, hard dribble and speed that he put defenses on their heels. His dad, Joe, was a former Division I point guard himself, and had taught Conor these dribbling techniques. Conor went on to have an excellent career at Division II Adelphi College in Long Island from 2015–2019. Conor's shining moment was at the Westchester County Center in 2015 in a Section 1 Class AA (NY's largest schools) semifinal game where, in storybook fashion, he had the ball in the waning seconds of a tied game, and he did something remarkable.

Conor circled with the ball toward half-court, *away* from the defense, before circling like a bull preparing for a final dash at a matador. But unlike the bull, who often ends being fooled as it dives into an empty cloth, Conor did not come up empty. He charged right back toward his defender *with his hard pounding dribble,* putting his defender on his heels, and elevated into a 17-foot pull-up jump shot that went swish for a 61–59 win! Don't dribble lethargically. Don't dribble weakly. Get some force in that dribble.

86. CATCH THE BALL WITH TWO HANDS!

It seems like a simple, obvious fundamental. Catching the ball. Of course. Yet I am amazed at how many players lack the fundamentally sound, clean, no-bobble, two-handed catch. Catch with two hands. Don't block the ball and knock it down only to then regain control. I recently coached three varsity players on the same team who used this method. One would block it down, and two others would try to catch the ball with one hand. Stretch your arms away from your body with your thumbs out at 10 and 2 o'clock. Make a diamond shape with your hands, but don't have your hands touching. Leave about four inches of space between your hands.

87. HOW TO SET AND USE SCREENS.

To set a screen, come to a loud *jump stop*. This eliminates moving screens. Do not readjust your screen and pick up an offensive foul. Interlock your left arm over your right wrist and keep that six inches away from your body—a Coach Bob Knight technique, and no team set or used screens better than his.

It is the job of the player using the screen to properly set up his cut. Go two steps away from a screen in order to better use an off-the-ball screen. When receiving a down screen, walk your defensive player under the rim before bursting out ready to use the screen. Change speeds. Go away slowly and come off the screen quickly; if a defender cheats up the inside, flair to the corner. If the defender trails you, curl to the elbow or middle of the paint.

When setting the screen for a pick-and-roll (an on-the-ball screen, as opposed to an off-the-ball screen), Coach Mike D'Antoni would have screeners contact half the body, the half closer to the basket (like Amar'e Stoudemire, who would often just tap and go to be fed with a slot bounce pass by Steve Nash). He did not teach the reverse-pivot box-out and roll that I recommend. Whether you tap and go or screen and reverse-pivot roll the key is *to not stand still.* You either roll or pop.

Coaching Bonus Tip:

Do not all allow on-ball screeners to stand still. Don't let your post screener get lazy. Demand that immediate roll or pop. No spectating.

88. SHOW ME $10 AND ASK FOR $5 CHANGE.

Backdoor cuts. Setting up the defense for your backdoor cut starts with you taking your defender away from the basket (lift them higher) with both arms up high and hands (all 10 fingers) asking for the ball. Push off your top foot (the foot closer to the sideline or half-court) and sprint toward the basket with one hand out (get that $5 change). Do not overplay your fake move away from the basket. The best backdoor moves are quite subtle and happen quickly, with just one step up and go.

89. FINISH YOUR CUTS.

If you begin a backdoor cut, do not stop halfway through, because your passer may end up throwing the ball away, not knowing your intentions. Don't expect a passer to read your mind. Any backdoor cut must end out the other side or in a short loop and post up. Cut with pace, and be ready to catch and make a play.

30-Second Timeout

WNBA AND THE FLU

In the spring of 2000, I started a scouting service that was really just me watching games from home, writing up WNBA reports, and mailing them out to teams. Lo and behold, I get a call from the Miami Sol, and I start scouting some games for them. Kevin Cook, associate head coach of the three-time WNBA champion Houston Comets likes my scouting reports as well, and hires me to write up reports for him. I am not doing it for the money, but rather to test myself and see what I can learn from the women's game. I come to love the execution of sets and admire the talents of the women in this emerging league.

It is the spring of 2001. The Nets, led by Jason Kidd, are making another late run into the playoffs. The WNBA season is just beginning, and I am enjoying watching the NY Liberty led by their star point guard, Teresa Weatherspoon. The league's premier act is the Houston Comets, led by Cynthia Cooper, Sheryl Swoopes, and Tina Thompson. They end up winning three straight titles, and I will end up completing two scouting reports for their associate head coach,

Kevin Cook, this particular summer. Because a Nets assistant coach/scout is involved with his playoff run, he is unable to do scouting assignments for the Miami Sol, and I get hired to scout some games in the interim. The pay is massive, for I receive $100 a game.

Miami sends me to scout the Houston Comets in Washington DC, and they fly me out and put me up in a nice hotel. That afternoon my sinuses feel completely jammed, but no big deal, probably just a cold. By the late afternoon my body is on fire, and my muscles are aching. Flu. Yikes. I am on the hook, and there is no way I am going to miss my assignment. A couple aspirin and I go across the street to the arena and visit the locker room, where I find Michael Jordan's Wizards locker. My favorite play from the Comets is out of a box set, where Cynthia Cooper dribble drags to the right side, Sheryl Swoopes diagonal up screens for Tina Thompson to the ball-side box, and the other post picks the picker, Swoopes, freeing her up for a top of the key three-point shot. The play execution and passing in the WNBA is something I admire and utilize in both boys' and girls' coaching situations. Since the players don't jump out of the building like some of the men in the NBA, it resembles the situations I more often found myself in coaching boys in high school.

I am about to begin a new chapter of my coaching career in 2023 as a varsity girls coach at Briarcliff High School in Briarcliff, NY. The WNBA and women's college game reveals greater female athleticism and basketball skill sets than ever before and serve as motivational forces for young girls. Exciting times.

90. BE VERBAL—NO SILENT MOVIES.

Players need to be verbal. Society is so used to texting that we can easily forget to talk on the floor. Not acceptable in basketball. Communication—loud, consistent communication—is vital to a team's connectedness on the court, especially when teams are facing crowd noise and other distractions. Connected teams win. When a coach makes an offensive play call, every player on the floor and on the bench should echo the call. Coaches may want to consider not only using loud verbal echoing but also various silent, visual signals that can be translated to the players in difficult environments like road, playoff games. Silent play calls may include a thumb to the chin, tapping a forehead, a high fist, and other gestures. The other players on the floor need to all repeat the nonverbal cue. On defense, yell *at switch, let me through, mine, tornado,* or *blitz,* as well as number calls such as *five* for man, *three* for 3-2 and more. During my last year at Putnam Valley, we switched from zone to man within a possession from a color call such as *purple!*

Coaching Exemplar: Coach George Gaine,

Tappan Zee High School.

Communication was one key element contributing to Tappen Zee's 2023 NY Class A state championship. George Gaine is a great coach, and his program excels at communication on the basketball court. The players echo calls with the bench players loudly joining in. Extensive use of additional, nonverbal signs helps them communicate their changing plays and sets in the loudest of environments.

Coaching Bonus Tip:

Stop every practice session where you feel there is insufficient communication. In addition, you must work out all these verbal and nonverbal calls in the preseason and practice them in summer and fall leagues.

91. DOWN FIVE, YOU DRIVE.

There are less than 90 seconds left in a game, or even less than 30 seconds left in a game, and you are down five as you cross half-court. You are thinking I must take a three; we don't have much time. Remember this fact: The defense does not want to give up a three-point shot when they are up five. You dribble into a rushed semi-challenged three and the ball clanks off the rim. Drive the ball and get a quick two. Remember this other factor: The opposing coach will be very angry at his own player if he fouls you for an old fashioned three-point play. Now you've cut the lead to three, and you look to pressure and steal the ball. When behind, you don't always have to get it all back immediately. If the same scenario presents a wide open three and you are a good shooter, then shoot it. However, don't force a bad three. Get a clean look and have an attack-the-rim mentality. Score. Timeout.

92. THERE AIN'T NO MAGIC DUST.

There are some very good sport-specific trainers and AAU coaches and programs, but getting better takes more than that. Most off-season travel teams practice twice a week, at most, except for the very high-level AAU teams. Players need to hear this message: Mom and Dad are paying good money. Don't practice two days per week and sit on the couch the rest of the time. Make 5,000 jump shots this summer. Make 2,000 foul shots. Work on the six moves I described in the Coach DeMello series on your own, and finish each move with a driving layup. Parents: No outside trainer has *magic dust* to sprinkle on your child. Balance and respect are critical. There are some great AAU opportunities offered to players, while allowing them to continue to meet school team obligations. If your child plays on a spring AAU team, make sure she is available for the school's team summer camp and summer league. Coaches don't have an infinite number of players to choose from, and when some are missing, the entire group suffers. Remember, your school coach earned that position through a serious hiring process, so don't disrespect the school coach. Those jobs aren't won so easily. And remember, *there ain't no magic dust.*

93. VISUALIZATION AND MENTAL CYBERNETICS.

Our various Olympic sports teams and individual athletes have used mental cybernetics to their advantage for years. These are mental exercises that consists in bringing your successes from past experiences into the present moment. There are studies that show that shooting and making foul shots in your mind can help you improve your overall shooting success when in an actual contest. As you lie in bed, visualize and make 20 foul shots before sleeping at night. See yourself going through your routine, hear the ball going through the net, and see it swish and move the net back and forth. Visualize being in a packed gym in a pressure situation, so that when these moments come upon you, you feel more ready and prepared for them. It truly works.

94. DON'T MAKE MISTAKE-MISTAKES.

All players make mistakes. It is inevitable. Delete. Press the delete button in your brain. Next play. Next play. Handle your mistakes like a champion. Keep your confidence. Have a next-play mentality. Refocus your efforts to make a positive impact on the next possession and beyond. Don't dwell on a mistake or show negative body language. Rick Pitino was the first coach I heard emphasize: *"No mistake-mistakes."* He realized that players make mistakes. Nobody is perfect. You will make mistakes. Get right back in the game mentally and keep giving focused effort.

95. POINT AND ACKNOWLEDGE YOUR PASSER.

If you receive a pass and finish with a score (or even miss), say *thank you* to the passer by pointing and giving an affirmative nod. Let good passers know that you appreciate their efforts and that you do not take their unselfishness for granted. The great Dean Smith teams of North Carolina were once known for this habit.

96. PLAYERS ARE NOT TO GET TECHNICAL FOULS.

On my first coaching assignment at the high school level, I watched how Coach Kelly handled a player getting a technical foul. He would sit that player out for a quarter or half of the next game with the threat of a game suspension for a repeat offense. This zero tolerance resulted in us not having to act punitively very often, because players knew not to get technicals. Coaches, let your players know that they are not to get technicals. Let them know that you are their voice. You may occasionally get a technical, if need be. But they are *not* to get technicals.

97. COACHES: NEVER LET A LOSS RUIN A SEASON.

This was taught to me by Coach Kelly in my very first year as an assistant high school coach at Rye. A high school season is often a rollercoaster ride, and even in the best of seasons, you are bound to have one mess of a game. You learn about the character of a team when it hits adversity. A young coach doesn't always realize this and may overreact after a bad effort. We had one such game at Putnam Valley, with a complete and utter collapse in the fourth quarter against a local rival team. An 18-point lead vanished, and we were outscored in the fourth by 19 points to lose by one. The opponent had a six-foot-eight center and went to a 1-3-1 zone, and frankly,

I did not do my best coaching job. On the way home I spoke with Coach Holford, and he said, "You went to the two-tight offense, right? The two tight?" No, I tried two other things that blew up.

The next practice was snowed out, and we met at a house to watch game tape. I told the players, *"This loss is on me. We will be just fine."* A few weeks later, we were cutting down the nets and heading to the County Center Final 4. Never let a loss ruin a season. A message to players who are true leaders: Don't dwell in negativity after a tough loss. Keep your teammates together and urge them to get right back on track. As for coaches, own up to mistakes with players. Stay off social media and pay no heed to gossip from people who have no stake in doing the work necessary to win.

98. MANAGE THE CRITICAL END-OF-QUARTER GAME.

Your teammate gains possession of the ball with 27 seconds left in the first quarter, lead passes to you with 20 seconds left, and you shoot the ball with 12 seconds left, miss, and the ball is pushed the other way for a quarter-ending, three-point make. What? No! No! This can't happen. We need to consistently win end of quarter situations. Think. We want to start offensive actions with about ten to twelve seconds left, shoot with five seconds left, so that we have an attempt for an offensive rebound and leave our opponent with two or three seconds left, limiting their reasonable chances for a final response. At worst, we must tie in the last 27 seconds of action. At best, we win 3–0, and we are just fine with winning 2–0, but to lose the 27-second game within a game when we started with possession is a *NO.*

99. KEEP TRACK OF THE TIME AND THE SCORE.

It is the second quarter of a tied game, and you are considered your team's best shooter. You get the ball in transition and shoot a wide-open three. Good shot? Yes, indeed. There is 1:42 left on the clock, and you are up seven, same location, and you get that ball. Should you shoot it this time? You must *know the time and the score,* and whether you are in the bonus or double bonus. Those are four things you should know. Seven points is not much of a lead in the era of the three-point shot. If you shoot and miss and the opponent scores, we now have a five- or even four-point game with a lot of time left. *Do not shoot!* Run clock. Space out. Catch and sight rim in case the defense gambles and fails to protect the rim, allowing an uncontested layup for a teammate. Twenty seconds later, they foul in a state of frustration. You go to the line with confidence and increase the lead to nine. Good players are always aware of the time and the score.

You are down two with 42 seconds left, and you know the opponent has to shoot within 35 seconds leaving you enough time with 7 seconds left. You don't commit a hurried foul, but instead trust you and your teammates to get a needed stop and rebound. Time and score. Always pay attention to the time and score.

100. COMPETE.

A message to all players. Coaches most desire players who compete. They want players who hate to lose and whose focus is the team and its success. Play to win. It is not about statistics; it is about *enjoying the experience* of competing to *WIN*. Team chemistry is so important to winning. Have the mentality that as a player, if I am not part of the solution, I am part of the problem.

I am by seven years the older brother to one of the most recognizable faces in college coaching, Dan McDonnell, head baseball coach at the University of Louisville. I remember him as a 10-year-old, shaking like a wind chime caught in a storm, facing a pitch in the bottom of the last inning, with a midget-baseball championship on the line. This was no ordinary championship game. The opposing team was coached by the NY Jets starting safety at the time, Shafer Suggs. This brought a lot of attention to our town's midget baseball league that year. Dan, of course, did not want to lose, or let his coach, me, or anyone else down. He squeezed out a hit to win the championship, and yes, big brother recorded every at bat. He batted 666 percent that year. No wonder he was shaking just a bit. Yes, sports are supposed to be fun, and Dan would soon learn to channel high pressure moments into joyous ones.

I remember Dan suffering from pain in his triceps area in high school and how this was going to possibly deter him from a junior varsity start as quarterback. So we both snuck into the Marriott Hotel in Tarrytown, NY, to use their hot tub to alleviate his pain (we had to improvise as best we could). He returned home, convinced he was ready for the next day's game. At 10 o'clock on that Saturday morning, he was receiving practice snaps from the center and dropping most of them before my father saw enough, and off to the hospital they went. We soon learned he had a broken arm, all along, and that was the reason he was unable to receive the center-quarterback exchange.

How much do you love to compete? AAU has so many games, there is often no chance for reflection: win two and lose one, win one and lose two. AAU. The games keep going on and on. Too often there is no time to reflect on how each player performed and whether the player or players competed in a fundamental fashion or with a cohesive, team approach. After a game or set of games, each player can reflect on how well he or she competed. Coaches, give the players feedback. Keep charts of rebounds and steals and much more. Feedback is so critical.

Coaches' Note:

When you have your team at an AAU event and have two games off between contests, do you let the players scatter? You have a captive audience. Don't waste that precious time. Tell players you have thirty minutes to report back, and then review the previous game and set the course for the next game. Go to a parking lot and walk through your fast break. Set a goal: We will complete one inbound from the 5-man to the 2-man at half-court, during this next game. Review key concepts like the burning hot coals and hitting the first open man or winning 50/50 balls. Review a chart that lists the rebounds gathered by each player. Simply never stop coaching.

101. ENJOY EVERY MOMENT OF THE JOURNEY.

Players, this book starts with you in mind, first and foremost. I've never won games with bad players. Players are the essential component in any season. This is such a great game, and I want all of you to enjoy it. Enjoy practicing with teammates and friends. Enjoy team activities together. Enjoy the competition and the excitement of games. Don't let losses take away your joy. Work harder to improve, and be a leader for your teammates. Embrace your role on the team. Be a willing student and learn from your coaches. Have an attitude of gratitude. Don't wait for blessings but *be the blessing* to others: your family, your teammates, and everyone you meet. Now, get the rock in your hands and work on your game. Think not only about playing harder but also about *playing smarter.* You have all these new ideas from this book.

Coaches, I see this book as an opportunity to refocus your attention on all the finer points and fundamentals of the game. When embraced and taught to players, they can make the difference between winning and losing, especially in tight games. Your opposing coaches all borrow the same plays off YouTube. What will give you the edge? Your ability to develop players individually, create a distinct style of team play, motivate and create a realistic dream or goal to achieve, and create a team that executes the type of fundamentals and concepts mentioned throughout this book. Have each player on your team purchase a copy of the book and use it as a resource so that everyone will *speak a common language.* Type up your own Top 10 guiding principles, laminate your list, and give your players your guiding manifesto.

It was most difficult coaching in the NY metro area at the height of the COVID-19 pandemic (the 2020–21 season). We had a varsity season with only nine games, and we played one opponent three times. We were so appreciative to have an opponent—any opponent! The feeling of respect, love, and true appreciation for sportsmanship and competition were never more heightened than during this time period.

Make practice and games fun. Enjoy the entire experience. Parents need to find joy in the glory of having a healthy child who has the opportunity to be a part of a team, no matter what her role. As for coaches, don't ever let anyone else knock you down and keep *you* from following your dreams. I've been the toast of one community and in another which was bereft of much talent, I was questioned robustly. You may just be in a terrible situation. Don't walk away from this great game. Reinvent yourself. Battle. Start again. There is *greatness* within *you.* You are great. Don't let a Twitter fool or upset parent make you believe differently. God bless.

Afterword

As coaches, we try to get a little better each year, while retaining our core beliefs about how to approach the game of basketball. I approach the game with humility and love to learn from anyone who has something to offer that makes analytical sense. Humility is key. As the game evolves, be open to growth. Don't take on too many new ideas and start anew each year, rather pick a few areas for tweaking and improvement and implement them.

Finally, it is not how much basketball *you, the coach, know,* but rather *what your players know* and integrate into their daily approach to the game that matters. You have to reinforce the concepts you value most, over and over and over again; otherwise, you will be tuned out either consciously or unconsciously by your players. You may feel like you have told a player to sight rim 199 times and that they still don't catch and sight rim before dribbling. The 200th time it might just sink in, so don't quit on your repetition and commitment to your values. The best coaches are teachers. Have fun and security in the knowledge that you are truly teaching the game. To teach the fundamentals of the game, one must be clear and persistent. Praise often; catch your players *doing right.* Be a teacher. Be a motivator. Be a leader.

Coaches, look for Volume 2: *55 Winning Boys' & Girls' Basketball Program Builders & Tactics: A Complete Coach's Guide to Running a Year-Round Program.* This book will be filled with practical, ready-to-implement ideas for coaches of all levels and focus upon unique, exciting team and program builders, developed especially for those coaches who want to try fresh, transformative ideas. Be on the lookout.

ACKNOWLEDGMENTS

Thank you to all the players I have been blessed to coach. I love all of you. I have never won a game without talented, dedicated, competitive players. My fond memories go well beyond the wins. I focus on the entire process of each season and the special times shared together. My wish is to see all my former players on a more regular basis and to reconnect with many as often as possible.

A huge thank you to my former assistant coaches and to a special colleague whom I assisted, Matt Simone at Horace Greeley High School. Mike Dutra, you were my longest-serving assistant. In a book of memories presented to me by the Putnam Valley community, you jokingly wrote of "six years and 100,000 phone calls" as a key memory of my insane imposition on your life. Michael, you were irreplaceable and so key to our PV success. Brad Grogan, Shawn Tarkington, John Taboada, and Owen and Xavier Lloyd, Jonas Solano, Frank Sileo, and CJ Lacosta brought their talents and served the players well. Phenomenal assistants along the journey who were *outstanding head coaches in their own right:* Chris DiCintio, Tom Brown, Steve Marcellino, Frank Kelly, Dave Fernandez, and John Rapaport. Congratulations to David Goldshore, former player and assistant coach who in the first year of his tenure at Staples HS (2022–23) advanced to the state final. Thank you to the "shot doctor," John Goldman, whose innovative driveway workouts were a sight to see. Lou DeMello's player-development training was a huge part of my ability to turn around Kennedy Catholic during our Covid year.

Team moms like Lisa Spittal and Cheryl Soto are a must for any coach trying to keep it all together. You made the experience more special for the boys.

Thank you to all my coaching peers in Section 1 and the NYCHSAA. I have such respect for you. The time and dedication you give to these developing youngsters does not ever match the financial compensation. We know that we don't coach for the money, yet fair compensation is welcome, because everyone has bills to pay.

Thank you to the officials who make their best efforts in a seemingly thankless environment. Too many are being pressed to officiate into their 70s because we don't have enough officials from the next generation. Know that you are respected and appreciated, for the game does not go on without you. It takes a lot of courage to go out and officiate in a playoff environment with the lights shining bright and fans viewing calls from one, and only one, perspective: their own team winning. As coaches, we only ask that you go into each game blind of any regional connection and give us your unbiased best, for in a game you are, in effect, our justice system. Players and coaches work too hard to even have to worry about whether they are getting a square deal. I know the vast majority of officials strive to give their best efforts.

To my colleagues: I highly recommend the Amateur Athletic Union, the preeminent youth athletic organization in the United States. I have been a proud member of the AAU for many years. Their many developmental opportunities and numerous AAU-sponsored competitions have extended my players' skills and enriched their basketball experience. AAU's mission is to foster good sportsmanship, as well as the physical, mental, and moral development of amateur athletes. Their motto: "Sports for All, Forever!"

In addition, I heartily endorse the Positive Coaching Alliance for their work in bringing greater humanity and professionalism to coaching. For information on their programs, visit https://positivecoach.org.

A huge thank you to Marty Nemecek who hired me for the most successful six years of my coaching career at Putnam Valley. Marty, you made it SO EASY to succeed. Thank you to John Ford, Gayle Simpson, Tracey Smith, Dom Tassone, and Jamie Block: dedicated, talented athletic directors. Thank you to Rich Silverstein for making my coaching experience at such a great Jewish school, Solomon Shecter, memorable and fun. Thank you to Chris Drosopoulos for my new start with girls' basketball and the opportunity to coach with my dear friend, Chris DiCintio. It is going to be a blast! Go Bears!

Thank you to my wife and girls, who shared me with my teams and my commitment to my passion. I hope that, through me, my daughters came to know the joy of finding a passion, a true love for something meaningful in their lives, and that they will find equally rewarding pursuits and interests.

Contact Mike McDonnell:

Email:swish33ny@gmail

Instagram: swish33basketball

LinkedIn: https://www.linkedin.com/in/michael-mcdonnell-51866526/

Facebook: https://www.facebook.com/profile.php?id=100094088610172